CW00967661

A PRIMER OF HANDLING THE NEGATIVE THERAPUETIC REACTION

Jeffrey Seinfeld

JASON ARONSON INC.
Northvale, New Jersey
London

This book was set in 11 pt. New Baskerville by Alabama Book Composition of Deatsville, AL and printed and bound by Book-mart Press, Inc. of North Bergen, NJ.

Library of Congress Cataloging-in-Publication Data

Seinfeld, Jeffrey.
    A primer of handling the negative therapeutic reaction / Jeffrey Seinfeld.
        p. cm.
    Includes bibliographical references and index.
    ISBN 0-7657-0363-7
        1. Psychotherapy—Complications.   2. Impasse (Psychotherapy)
3. Psychotherapist and patient.   I. Title.

RC580.5 .S4167 2002
616.89'14—dc21

                            2002020064

Printed in the United States of America on acid-free paper. For information and catalog write to Jason Aronson Inc., 230 Livingston Street, Northvale, NJ 07647-1726, or visit our website: www.aronson.com

To Dr. George Frank who,
as a mentor, provided much inspiration for this book.
To Kasey Sheehan, my production editor,
and the Jason Aronson staff for the splendid work
and time that was put into this manuscript.

Contents

Introduction

The negative therapeutic reaction is among the most pernicious problems among therapists of all levels of experience. Beginning clinicians are likely to feel that the patient's worsening condition is the result of their inexperience, inadequacy, and lack of skill. Experienced clinicians are likely to feel that their training and previous treatment encounters offer little help or guidance. This volume presents questions by students of this author concerning problems that typically arise around the negative therapeutic reaction. Our work with clients is dialogical and this book that follows spirit as the narrative is comprised of dialogues about clinical problems.

Historically, the negative therapeutic reaction was viewed as the patient's response to improvement from treatment. It was believed that unconscious guilt, envy, and the need to suffer prompted the patient to defeat the therapist in his or her efforts to help. Therapists experienced in guilt, frustration, anger, and resignation as the patient's condition seemed to get worse as a result of treatment. In turn, the clinician's sense of futility became an obstacle in the effort to contain the patient's despair.

As psychoanalytic theory became more relational, the question of the therapist's involvement became central. Not only do patients induce countertransference, but the countertransference might unconsciously contribute to the negative therapeutic reaction. The patient's worsening condition must be understood in the context of the therapeutic relationship and not exclusively as the pathology of the patient. At the same time, certain patients will be more likely to experience a negative reaction because of their pathology. The negative therapeutic reaction occurs between the patient and therapist and not only in the patient.

The author fully acknowledges the profound difficulties in working in this area, but also believes that the negative therapeutic reaction provides significant opportunity to bring about positive change. By allowing the patient to give full expression to the bad object transference, and by honestly examining when counter-transference reactions might, in fact, fit the characteristics of the bad object, the therapist can help the patient exorcise his or her internal demons.

The author presents a treatment approach that resembles the Chinese martial art of Tai Chi Chuan. In this soft ancient art, one yields to the energy and strength of the other and makes use of the momentum. In managing the negative therapeutic reaction, the clinician should not attempt to thwart or block it, but instead invite its full expression and make use of it as an opportunity to enable the patient to separate from bad internal objects.

I

The Historic View
of the Negative
Therapeutic Reaction

Question: What is the negative therapeutic reaction?

Seinfeld: The phrase was adopted to describe a situation in which the client's condition worsened not despite the treatment but actually because of it. It was assumed that the clinician was generally conducting the treatment correctly but that the client reacted adversely. Freud, Abraham, and Klein were the pioneers in discovering and working with clients suffering from negative therapeutic reactions. They were pessimistic about the efficacy of treatment but believed that the study of the negative therapeutic reaction could yield significant understanding of the dynamics of severe pathology. The therapeutic relationship provides the clinician with a live opportunity to witness the exacerbation of the client's condition. In recent times, it is no longer assumed that the clinician's technique is correct. For instance, as therapists have had considerably more experience working with severely disturbed clients, it has become apparent that the classical

Freudian technique may not be effective or may even exacerbate the symptoms of patients with self disorders or pre-oedipal problems. Freud, Abraham, and Klein all worked with some variation of the classical technique, which may provide at least a partial answer to the question of why they were so pessimistic.

In recent times, there is greater focus on addressing the impact of trauma, not only on transference but also on the countertransference factors that contribute to the negative therapeutic reaction. A further important consideration is the intersubjective nature of the therapeutic relationship.

Question: How was the negative therapeutic reaction originally recognized?

Seinfeld: Sigmund Freud (1916) originally described the negative therapeutic reaction in his work with a young woman. He stated that she rebelled against her family by running away from home. Later she met a young artist who wished to marry her. It seemed that just when her life circumstance had begun to improve, she neglected the home she and her lover shared, imagined that her husband's family was persecuting her, and then succumbed to a chronic and severe mental illness. Freud attributed the young woman's breakdown to guilt. He also noted that in the case of the wolf-man, the patient experienced transitory negative therapeutic reactions when the analysis progressed.

Freud's explanation assumes that the clinician and the people in the person's life are good enough objects and that the patient's breakdown is exclusively the result of fear and guilt over success. In a more contemporary outlook, the question could be raised as to whether the clinician's countertransference could block him or her from recognizing that the persons in the patient's life situation may be subtly mistreating or persecuting her, and she fears asserting herself openly and thereby becomes ill as a way to run away from an untenable situation. Another possibility would be that the patient's successful life situation is actually a false self-adaptation, and the patient's true self protests by the break-down. These considerations do not prove that Freud's explanation is wrong, but clinicians today would not necessarily be as quick to assume that the persons in the client's life or the therapist are good enough objects or that the patient's conventionally successful life is necessarily emotionally fulfilling. One can see that there is a certain cultural bias in the case vignettes' assumptions as to what is a good and successful life.

There are certain people who behave in a quite peculiar fashion during the work of analysis. When one speaks hopefully to them or expresses satisfaction with the progress of the treatment, they show signs of discontent, and their condition invariably becomes worse. One begins by regarding this as a defiance and as an attempt to prove their superiority to the physician, but later one comes to take a deeper and juster view. One becomes convinced not only that such people cannot accept any praise or appreciation but also that they react inversely to the progress of the treatment. Every partial solution ought to result, and in other people does result, in an improvement.

Freud (1924) stated that the negative therapeutic reaction occurred when he spoke hopefully or expressed satisfaction with the progress of the treatment. The patients showed signs of discontent, such as missing sessions, coming late, not paying, or reporting an exacerbation of symptoms. Freud at first attributed their negative reaction to defiance and an effect to defeat the clinician. He stated that interventions that resulted in improvement for most patients have the opposite negative effect.

Question: What factors did Freud believe contribute to the negative therapeutic reaction?

Seinfeld: Freud (1924) believed that the negative therapeutic reaction resulted from the patient's unconscious need for punishment. The sadism of the superego and the masochism of the ego complemented one another in the negative therapeutic reaction. The patient suffers from a severe sense of guilt and sadomasochism derived from the death instinct. Freud (1937) remained quite pessimistic about treatment, possibly because of his attributing the negative therapeutic reaction to the death instinct.

Freud's study of the negative therapeutic reaction was of great significance in the development of his structural theory (id, ego, and superego). The masochism of the ego led him to the conviction that part of the ego's defensive structure is unconscious, and unconscious guilt led him to the discovery of the unconscious aspects of a third structure of the psyche, the superego.

Question: Do envy and narcissism play a role in the negative therapeutic reaction?

Seinfeld: Karl Abraham was renown for working with severely disturbed and depressed clients. He (1919) also recognized negative reactions to progress and pointed to problems of unconscious envy and narcissism. He described patients who begrudge the therapist any recognition of progress, strive to feel superior to the therapist, and want to do the treatment on their own. It was believed that accepting the clinician's help aroused fear and envy.

The patient does not feel a close dependence on the clinician as a separate other but instead wants to become one with the clinician. They adopt the therapist's interests and like to occupy themselves with psychoanalysis as a science instead of allowing it to act on them as a way of helping. They tend to exchange roles as a child plays at being a parent. They instruct the clinician as if they are the supervisors and imagine that science will be especially advanced by their treatment. Abraham noted that such patients feel superior to their clinicians, provoke arguments about technique, and are preoccupied with ideas that serve their narcissism.

It is interesting to note that Abraham's vivid clinical description focuses on the client's narcissism and envy as radical obstacles to transference and progress, whereas currently this clinical material would be understood as evidence of a strong self-object narcissistic transference (self-psychology) or a part-object transference (object relations) in which the patient mobilized split-off, hidden, internalized object relations, thereby creasing an opportunity for working through.

Question: Does the negative therapeutic reaction reenact infantile experience?

Seinfeld: Melanie Klein, who had been analyzed by Abraham, adopted his view concerning the importance of envy and narcissism but developed her own outlook on how early object relations are enacted in the transference. Klein (1957) views the negative therapeutic reaction as an enactment of the early feeding situation. She emphasized that oral envy exists at the beginning of life. The most severe negative reactions occur when envy is split off and hidden because of the primitive defenses directed against it. Klein (1946) described the primitive defenses as splitting, idealization, devaluation, and projective identification. Clinical examples and definitions of these defenses will be provided later. The patient may also project split-off envy into the therapist and then fear retaliation.

Klein viewed the negative therapeutic reaction as derived from the death instinct. The split-off envy manifests itself clinically as an inability to accept with gratitude interpretations that are perceived in some part of the patient's mind as helpful. She (1957) stated that the helpful interpretation is destroyed through criticism so that it is no longer perceived to be something nourishing. The patient experiences the transference/countertransference in the context of feeding and endeavors to spoil or destroy the potentially good breast because of envy.

James Grotstein describes how the infant of Kleinian theory must save itself from self-destructiveness (the death instinct) by directing its aggression outward toward the maternal breast. Therefore, as the infant later maturationally integrates the good and the bad part-object breasts into a whole object, there is the phantasy that it is destroying both the good and the bad object breast. The infant eventually experiences guilt as a result of its phantasy of injuring or destroying the good breast because it destroyed the object so as not to destroy itself. Grotstein describes this Kleinian dilemma as one of original sin.

Question: What is meant by destructive narcissism?

Seinfeld: Herbert Rosenfeld (1987) elaborated on the Kleinian theory of the negative therapeutic reaction. Rosenfeld stated that the persecutory bad objects, in the form of destructive narcissism, attack positive libidinal object relations. These destructive and omnipotent aspects of the psyche are disguised or hidden but play an essential role in preventing or destroying good object relations. Patients may feel indifferent to the external world. They may feel that they have created and given life to themselves and can meet their own needs. They may even prefer to die, deny the fact of their birth, and destroy any potential for help rather than depend on the clinician. Self-destructive acting out may be idealized as an answer to one's problems. There is a distinction between narcissism that is healthy and that provides self-enhancement and narcissism that idealizes the destructive aspects of the self.

Rosenfeld draws on the metaphor of an internal gang of thugs treating the patient as a recalcitrant or disloyal gang member to describe internal persecutory objects. As members of a gang idealize one another, the leader, the gang as a whole, and its destructive actions, the patient idealizes his or her persecutory objects and their destructive acting out. Rosenfeld states that the patient does not experience the ganglike status of persecutory objects as a metaphor or symbol but rather as something that feels real and frightening. It is the psychotic part of the personality that undergoes the negative therapeutic reactions.

Question: What is the relationship between the negative therapeutic reaction and clinical diagnosis?

Seinfeld: The negative therapeutic reaction is not particularly and directly related to any one specific clinical diagnosis. The severe negative therapeutic reactions are associated generally with severe disorders, such as psychoses, borderline and schizoid states, severe narcissistic personalities, severe trauma, and depression. However, there are milder forms of negative therapeutic reactions that could occur with milder or less severe disorders. It is more useful to think of the negative therapeutic reaction occurring in the psychotic part of the personality.

Question: What is the psychotic and the nonpsychotic parts of the personality?

Seinfeld: British psychoanalysts, whether they are Kleinian or object relations (the difference will be discussed later), believe

7

that a psychotic core is ubiquitous to personality. Wilfred Bion described this phenomenon comprehensively. He argued that everyone has both psychotic and nonpsychotic parts of the personality. A psychotic part of the personality does not imply a diagnosis of psychoses. A neurotic personality has a hidden psychotic component, and a psychotic personality has a hidden sane or neurotic component. In writing about psychotic functioning, Freud stated that the psychotic hates and attacks reality because of frustration of the instinctual drives. Bion's important contribution is that the psychotic part of the personality not only hates and attacks reality but also hates and attacks the perceptual apparatus and ego functioning that relate to reality. Bion describes attacks on the capacity to think, to understand, and to make corrections. These attacks result in the patient's falling into a psychic state termed *K* (knowledge). The patient literally cannot think straight and appears to be dumber than he or she is. Bion stresses that such patients do not learn from experience. An example would be a patient who repeatedly behaves in a fashion that results in destructive consequences but does not appear to make the obvious connection between his or her action and the consequence. Bion's ideas suggest that the patient may be unconsciously and silently attacking the connection. In the negative therapeutic reaction, there are silent, split-off, hidden attacks on the perpetual apparatus by the psychotic fact of the personality.

Question: What role, if any, might the therapist play in the negative therapeutic reaction?

Seinfeld: Sandor Ferenczi was an analyst who lived and worked in Budapest. He was among the first analysts to work with persons subject to trauma and to recognize its full impact. He is also considered an important forerunner of British object relations theory and self-psychology. Ferenczi eloquently argued that if a patient was not treatable, it was because the therapist or therapy had not devised the necessary knowledge or effective means of intervention. Ferenczi was renown for taking on the most difficult of patients. In working with patients considered untreatable by the standard classical Freudian approach, Ferenczi engaged in original but unorthodox experiments.

Ferenczi worked with individuals who had been subject to trauma, originally with traumatized soldiers as a director of a special war neurosis clinic in Budapest and later with females subject to sexual abuse and incest. He became aware that trauma resulted in splitting and dissociation, leaving the patient overwhelmed by infantile and unconscious material.

Ferenczi (1933) drew parallels between the child traumatized by the hypocrisy of adults, the soldier traumatized by the hypocrisy of war, and the mentally ill traumatized by the hypocrisy of society. He hypothesized that the traumatized person went through a breakdown of defense, resulting in the patient surrendering to the traumatic circumstances and suffering dissociation and depersonalization. The patient developed the uncanny ability to withdraw outside herself and to view the abuser and the situation from a detached perspective. In this state, the patient could view the abuser as sick or mad and sometimes even try to cure or help the abuser. Ferenczi was the first to describe how abused children sometimes become therapists to their own parents and are often strikingly altruistic. He believed that the patient could suffer a similar trauma at the hands of a too rigid or distant therapist. When theory is applied dogmatically or the therapist denies his or her countertransference or when the patient is considered untreatable, the therapist inflicts a trauma on the patient that reawakens the traumas of the patient's past.

Ferenczi was interested in the relationship between the negative therapeutic reaction and early trauma. Freud, Abraham, and

Klein ultimately attributed the negative therapeutic reaction to the death instinct. Ferenczi was the first analyst to emphasize trauma as a central contributing factor. He did not explicitly focus on the negative therapeutic reaction in his writing, but his description of patients experiencing overwhelming infantile anxiety, terror, and despair clearly fit the classical descriptions of the negative therapeutic reaction. Once the negative reaction was attributed to early trauma and not an innate death instinct, it stood to reason that the therapist could inadvertently and easily traumatize the vulnerable patient and reawaken the earlier trauma. Ferenzi's argument was that the classical technique, when done correctly, could traumatize the patient. It is likely that Ferenczi's work is the basis for the current view that the negative therapeutic reaction may often be attributed to the therapeutic relationship and not only the patient.

Question: What was Ferenczi's experimental approach in working with the negative therapeutic reaction?

Seinfeld: It is interesting to note that Ferenczi's original approach was probably influenced by gender factors. He first worked with males traumatized by combat and modified classical technique in the direction of prohibitions and frustrations. This active technique consisted of the therapist restricting the patient from nail biting, head scratching, smoking, and even behavior outside the session, such as sexual or masturbatory activities. Ferenczi had recognized that free association as practiced in classical analysis often did not result in the patient remembering preverbal trauma. His technique sought to bring to the patient's consciousness preverbal experience that was not available through free association. It was felt that the preverbal tensions were finding release through the nonverbal actions described previously.

10

By prohibiting such actions, Ferenczi hoped that the tensions would have no recourse but would find release through verbal expression. Thus, Ferenczi originally remained faithful to the classical analytic idea of verbalizing and not enacting psychic conflict.

When Ferenczi began working with female traumatized patients, his technique changed from one of prohibition to one of support. He believed that the child's mind was originally whole but that inevitable traumas throughout development left it split and divided. He stated that the therapist needed to provide support and encouragement to reach the split-off selves. Only with the active support and caring of the therapist would the adult patient feel safe enough to risk the remembrance and reliving of early trauma. Ferenczi reached the conclusion that the therapist's interventions may not be expressed in a language that the patient understands. The patient may experience intellectual interpretations as abandonment if the patient is seeking support and encouragement. There is a danger that the therapist and patient will speak at cross-purposes in a confusion of tongues between adult and child. Ferenczi's work is also a forerunner to a cultural hermeneutic outlook that emphasizes that therapist and client can fall into a confusion of tongues if they are speaking from different cultural contexts, especially if the therapist is from a culture valuing the word and the client is from a culture valuing action. In a later chapter, I will describe how such a cultural confusion of tongues partially contributed to a negative therapeutic reaction.

Ferenczi questioned Freud's belief that the severely disturbed patient did not develop transference. He argued that with such patients, the therapist must first experience a positive counter-transference to elicit the patient's positive transference. The therapist's unconscious negative countertransference might elicit the patient's negative transference or even might initially experience a negative transference toward the therapist, evoking an

11

unconscious negative countertransference response. This response could in turn elicit a negative therapeutic reaction from the client. Or, from the opposite standpoint, the therapist may experience a negative countertransference toward the client, evoking a negative therapeutic reaction to the client.

Question: If the negative therapeutic reaction is evoked by the response or attitude of the clinician, is it truly a negative therapeutic reaction, or is it simply a real response?

Seinfeld: The term *negative therapeutic reaction* implies that the progress of treatment triggers a particular destructive dynamic in the client. The nature of that dynamic will be defined in the next chapter. If a patient has been traumatized and is vulnerable to being retraumatized and the therapist's approach, attitude, or response awakens the trauma, it is still understood that the patient has the dynamic associated with the negative therapeutic reaction and is threatened by the overall progress of the treatment. This situation differs from a patient's responding negatively to a mistake or negative response on the part of the therapist.

Question: What is the nature of the trauma reawakened in the negative therapeutic reaction?

Seinfeld: Ferenczi's outlook anticipated current object relations theory and can be viewed as an important framework in which to understand the dynamics described by object relations theory. Ferenczi described tenderness as a pre-oedipal register of experience. Tenderness includes oral gratification, kissing, cuddling, tactile closeness, and soothing words. These feelings express infantile sexuality but do not become urgent, greedy, or desperate unless excited by overstimulating or abusive behavior on the part of the adult. If a child's sexuality is excessive, it is likely to be complicated or grafted on by the overstimulating behavior of adults. Ferenczi termed this adult overstimulating sexuality passion, that is, the oedipal or post-oedipal register of phallic or genital experience. If the child expresses a desire for tenderness but the adult responds passionately, the language of passion is grafted on to the language of tenderness. The parent may provoke the language of passion by being overly stimulating, overly frustrating, or both.

As will be seen, Ferenczi's views anticipate current object relations theory. The language of tenderness implies that the individual is seeking attachment. The notion that the overstimulating parent excites the child's natural sensuality is identical to the concept of the exciting object. The fact that overly frustrating behavior on the part of the parent is also pathogenic brings to mind the concept of the rejecting object. The child's language of passion and guilt is indicative of the child's having internalized the parental reactions. The abusive parent often denies guilt about abusing the child, but the child is attuned to the unconscious guilt and identifies with the parent out of loyalty. The therapist's aim is to enable the patient to separate from the identification with the parents' guilt. It was to Ferenczi's credit that he recognized the patient's loyalty to the abusive object. This phenomenon is central to object relations theory's understanding of the negative therapeutic reaction. Ferenczi could not explain the dynamics underlying the loyalty factor. Ferenczi's technique of therapy was therefore quite limited because he could not effectively address this dynamic. It was left to object relations to develop a theory of the personality based on this loyalty to objects regardless of whether they are good or bad to the child.

13

II

Object Relations and the Negative Therapeutic Reaction

Thus far, we have reviewed the negative therapeutic reaction from the contexts of classical theory and the challenge of Sandor Ferenczi. Classical theory attributed the negative reaction to the death instinct, and Ferenczi attributed it to trauma. Ferenczi's views imply an intersubjective approach to the negative reaction in that the traumatized patient is highly vulnerable to a reawakening of the trauma if he or she suffers disappointment at the hands of the therapist. Ferenczi also presented a basic outline of the dynamics of these patients.

Ferenczi is considered a forerunner and anticipator of British object relations theory, which provides a comprehensive framework for understanding the negative therapeutic reaction.

Question: What is object relations theory?

Seinfeld: Object relations theory considers the individual as basically a social animal who develops individuality within the context of human relations. Object relations theorists describe this phenomenon with the phrase "libido is object seeking." Freud believed that libido is ultimately seeking pleasure and tension reduction. Classical theory stated that the object is a means or signpost to libidinal pleasure and discharge. British object relations theory believes that libidinal pleasure is the means or signpost of attachment to the object.

Classical theory also assumed that energy and structure are separate, based on the nineteenth-century Helmholtzian scientific view. Thus, Freud conceived of a structured ego without its own energy and a structureless id—a reservoir of instinctual drive energy. W. R. D. Fairbairn (1941), a major theorist of British object relations, based his theory of dynamic structure on Albert Einstein's twentieth-century scientific view that energy and structure are inseparable. Thus, Fairbairn conceived of a whole ego with its own energy. Thus, it is not libido but rather a libidinally inclined ego that is object seeking.

Question: How is personality understood?

Seinfeld: The personality is referred to as the self. At first, it is pristine and undifferentiated but has potential for wholeness. This self has a preconception of the object and is prewired to seek attachment. The self also consists of internal objects and the affects associated with them. The classical conception of an ego comprised of functions is also understood as a part of the self.

Question: What is an internal object?

Seinfeld: The patient's experience of being possessed by bad objects suggests that such objects are experienced by the clients as demonic. James Grotstein (1985) states that the internal world of objects is experienced by the client as a world of demons, monsters, spirits, ghosts, and so forth and not as static, nondynamic representations or images. The term *object* is generally used to refer to external persons and internal objects and is in fact semantically accurate in relationship to internal objects. The infant experiences the mother not only as an object of its needs but also as a subject. The infant recognizes and relates to the mother's changing facial expressions, changing voice, and smile, all of which exhibit her alive, spontaneous subjectivity. There are inevitable occurrences in which the infant will experience the caregiver's subjectivity as threatening and frustrating. The fact that the caregiver has needs and interests and relates to people separate from the infant who is entirely dependent on her gives rise to separation anxiety. Early experiences of deprivation and frustration are experienced by the infant as rejection and loss of primary love; deprivation results in the experience of psychic emptiness based on the biological experience of emptiness and hunger. Elsewhere, I (1991) have described this phenomenon as the empty core. This is not a static, spatial state but rather a psychic hunger to incorporate part-objects to fill the void. Through internalization, the object is stripped of her wholeness, subjectivity, and freedom and is transformed into a thinglike object. However, this thinglike object exacts its revenge by having a life of its own and possessing, tormenting, and persecuting its possessor. One initially possesses the object but is then possessed by it.

Question: How is an internal object manifested in conscious everyday life?

Seinfeld: A common example is that of internal dialogues. For instance, one quarrels with someone and afterward continues the quarrel in one's own mind. One is saying everything one ever wanted to say to the other and then imagines the other's response. In one's imagination, the other is giving as good as it is getting and takes on a life of its own. The affect involved is not different than if one were actually quarreling with another although one knows the quarrel is now imaginary. In fact, when one again meets the actual other person, he or she may seem not as bad as the internal counterpart. In this situation, the internal dialogue is a reflection of an unconscious relationship to a bad object.

Another example is irrational self-hatred and persecution. For instance, a patient berates him- or herself for being unattractive, unworthy, poor, selfish, or inadequate. Either the patient may be attacking an internal bad object he or she is identified with or the persecutory attack may reflect the bad object attacking oneself.

A patient always arrived late for sessions, then criticized herself for the lateness. The self-criticism seemed as much a part of her symptom as the lateness itself. The therapist started to feel that she might come late to give herself a reason to berate herself. On one occasion she described how in her childhood her mother brought her late to play dates, school, doctor appointments, and so forth. Thus, by coming late for sessions she reenacted how her mother always brought her places late and had difficulty letting her go. She denied feeling angry at her mother in her childhood, but her self-berating told a different story.

Question: Are internal objects always bad?

Seinfeld: Fairbairn (1943) believed only bad objects need to be internalized because this process is synonymous with attempting to control and transform a bad object into a good one. Bad objects are unconscious and repressed dynamic structures of the personality. What are referred to as good objects are conscious, pleasurable memories of good experiences with others. Good objects are important in enabling the child to tolerate separation from the caregiver. If there has not been good enough experience to internalize, the individual has no choice but to fill the void of separation with bad objects. As Fairbairn stated, a bad object is better than no object.

Question: Are internal objects exact replicas of the external persons they are based on?

Seinfeld: No. The infant constructs the internal object based on the external other. This construction inevitably results in a degree of distortion. The internal object may be more tantalizing or rejecting than its external counterpart because the infant splits the object into exclusive, exciting, and rejecting components and projects its own excitement and feelings of rejecting into the object. The infant also interprets its experience with the other in the context of its cognitive and emotional developmental level.

Question: How does object relations theory describe the internal world?

Seinfeld: Fairbairn (1944) conceived of his endopsychic structural theory, which provides a powerful explanatory model for the psychodynamics of the negative therapeutic reaction.

Grotstein (1985) described Fairbairn's endopsychic structure as an internal hell the patient is trapped within. It is comprised of split-off selves relating with hypnotic submission and worshiping loyalty toward intimidating, exciting, and rejecting objects. There is an infantile, needy libidinal self-relating to an exciting but nongratifying object and an antilibidinal internal saboteur self identified with a rejecting object. The antilibidinal self is a reservoir of memories of mistrust and is rejecting his or her own needs as he or she expects the world to inevitably reject and disappoint him or her. If someone acts kindly or caring toward the child and excites its dependency needs, the child feels certain this person is attempting to lure him or her into dependence and later disappointment. This situation reflects the antilibidinal self-identification with the rejecting object in rejecting the libidinal ego's need for the exciting object. The object is split into three parts: ideal, exciting and rejecting objects. The self also splits itself into three parts, and the subself relates to a corresponding part object. Thus, the libidinal self-exciting object and the antilibidinal self-rejecting object are split off and repressed, leaving a conscious central self relating to the ideal object, which is projected onto the external world.

Question: What function does the endopsychic structure serve?

Seinfeld: Object relations theory conceives of the individual as attempting to remain in contact with an object. Even when individuals distance themselves, they are doing so not only because they fear intimacy but also because distance allows the individual to remain in contact with a tolerable level of anxiety. One has only to think of the adolescent or young adult who never gets along with his or her family but moves away and gets along better at a distance. Fairbairn's endopsychic structural theory is conceived to explain this type of phenomenon. The all-good, idealized object is projected onto the external world and related to by the central conscious self, while the negative, exciting, frustrating, and rejecting selves and objects are split off and repressed. The individual is thereby able to remain in contact with the needed idealized outer world by repressing and splitting off negative frustrating experience that would threaten or interfere with one's relationship to the outer world. This splitting allows the patient to see the world through rose-colored glasses. However, one does so in a superficial, constricted, affectless fashion if one takes this dynamic to the extreme. It must be emphasized that Fairbairn sees this schizoid dynamic as something everyone does to some extent because the world is inevitably difficult and frustrating. Classical theory considers idealization a defense against aggression and guilt. Object relations theory does not deny the defensive aspect of idealization but also stresses its positive function for object relations.

Question: How does the endopsychic theory relate to the negative therapeutic reaction?

Seinfeld: The endopsychic structural theory serves as a powerful explanatory model for the negative therapeutic reaction. It must be remembered that the three respective selves—the central self, the libidinal self, and the antilibidinal self—are not static entities but instead are different ways that the psyche can function at the same time either consciously or unconsciously. As the patient becomes attached to the therapist, the antilibidinal self attempts to crush, attack, and destroy the needy, infantile libidinal self and the therapist to whom it turns for help. This hatred of dependence, on the part of the antilibidinal self, is the basic source of the negative therapeutic reaction. The antilibidinal self interprets dependence as weakness. The patient feels it is dangerous to allow him- or herself to feel in need and weak and to turn to someone for help since help will not be forthcoming. Thus, the antilibidinal self perpetuates the weakness of the personality by its active persecution and rejecting of a relationship that could eventually strengthen the personality. The antilibidinal self's resistance may be evident or hidden.

A male patient was becoming involved in treatment and beginning to see how his early family life stunted his mental growth. After a particularly productive session, he dreamt he was going to the clinic and his father stood before the door blocking his way. In subsequent sessions, the patient felt less motivated and enthusiastic. In this instance, loyalty toward the bad object was the source of the negative reaction. Antilibidinal reactions may also be more subtle and hidden. A patient may begin to trust and depend on the clinician's help when a hidden resistance starts up, gains in strength, and results in the patient feeling blocked and depressed and unable to be as involved as he or she consciously wishes.

Question: What are the motives for the antilibidinal self identifying with the rejecting object?

Seinfeld: Harry Guntrip (1969) states that when the antilibidinal self feels identified with the rejecting persecutory object, the patient is taking on the personality of the powerful figures in his or her early childhood. Thus, the patient counteracts the basic feeling of ego weakness by temporarily identifying with the bad powerful objects.

The therapist expressed empathy toward an adolescent female expressing self-hatred and acts of self-mutilation. The therapist said, "It must have been so frightening seeing the blood flow from your arm." She replied, "You don't understand. At the moment I

22

identified myself as the one attacking and hating myself, not the one being attacked and hated. As I saw the flow of blood, I felt powerful, invulnerable."

Another powerful source of the negative therapeutic reaction is the relationship to the exciting object. These patients are subject to split-off and repressed object hunger. There is an intense need to incorporate and merge with the object. The oral wish to devour the object results in a fear of being devoured. The early infant caregiver relationship is experienced through the medium of feeding; thus, the patient's attitude toward food may express his or her attitude toward early objects. Patients experiencing bingeing episodes with food, alcohol, or drugs may be expressing a displaced wish to devour the object. Patients fearing being devoured often report episodes of claustrophobia. They may express fears of engulfment in dreams of drowning, being buried alive, being swallowed up by quicksand, or being eaten by wild animals. There may be a fear of being trapped in relationships, in a job, or in a steady abode.

A patient sat silently. He said he feared speaking because he felt that if he expressed something of substance, the therapist would devour it and he would lose something valuable. The patient said, "I'm hungry, so I imagine that you are. If you discover I have something of value, you will want it for yourself."

The patient who pushes away the object and crushes his or her own needs may then feel as if the object is going away or rejecting in a rapid oscillation of exciting and rejecting object transferences. The exciting object transference evokes a fear of abandonment.

The patient may endeavor to utilize idealization and repress and split-off bad objects to remain in contact at a safe distance. This dynamic also allows the patient to remain in contact while simultaneously establishing a sense of separateness. If the libidinal self were to express its intense needs for the exciting object, there is the danger that the disappointment and frustration could be so great that ensuing rage could destroy the object. The patient may also feel that his or her love and need to be loved are so devouring as to be destructive. Fairbairn (1941) stated that the schizoid believes his or her love is destructive, while the depressive believes his or her hate is destructive. In the transference situation, the need for the exciting object results in a fear of merger, triggering the distancing identification with the rejecting object, resulting in fear of separation and object loss. Thus, the patient is on a rapid oscillation of exciting and rejecting object transference. If the patient separates from either bad object, there is terror of the loss of the subself relating to the bad object. Thus, the ultimate source of the negative therapeutic reaction is the loyal tie to the bad object.

Question: Why is the child loyal to its bad objects?

Seinfeld: As Fairbairn (1943) stated, the child needs and knows the parent it has. A bad object is better than no object. Fairbairn worked for many years in a clinic in the slums of Edinburgh with sexually and violently abused children. Time and again, these youngsters internalized the abusing parent and blamed themselves for the ill treatment they had suffered. Fairbairn concluded that the child idealized the external parent and incorporated the badness of the parent in order to protect the needed relationship. He said it is safer for the child to feel like a sinner in a universe ruled by God than a saint in a universe ruled by the devil. Furthermore, the child believes that it only has to behave and become good, and the parent would be transferred into a good object. Fairbairn described this dynamic as the moral defense.

Question: How does the patient separate from bad objects?

Seinfeld: D. W. Winnicott (1963) emphasizes the positive function that aggression serves in separating from objects. Winnicott describes the child as experiencing the subjective, omnipotent illusion that the object or caregiver is under its absolute control. He refers to the object in this situation as a subjective object. The child destroys the object as he or she experiences the object as separate and outside its control. The survival of the real person on whom the subjective object is based is crucial. As the child destroys the phantasyzed object, it discovers that the real object survives and is not the same as the phantasyzed object. Thus, the child discovers externality and distinguishes the objectively perceived real object from the subjective object of phantasy. In the negative therapeutic reaction, the patient verbalizes the negative reaction to the therapist, phantasyzes that he or she has destroyed the therapist, and gradually discovers that the real therapist survives.

Fairbairn (1943) states that for the patient to release the bad objects from the unconscious, the therapist has to be a good object in reality. The patient's destruction of the object is in the context of the activation of the bad object transferences. The paradox is that the therapist attempts to be a good enough, supportive object by accepting the patient's projection of the bad object without retaliating or withdrawing. By surviving the negative therapeutic reaction, the therapist allows the patient the opportunity to integrate good and bad part objects in the transference.

Question: What are some of the countertransference issues that occur in working with the negative therapeutic reaction?

Seinfeld: The patient unconsciously endeavors to re-create the emotional climate of early object relation in the relationship to the therapist. H. Racher (1968) studied therapist's countertransference reactions. The therapist may respond by identifying with the patient's internal objects (complementary identification) or with the patient's self (concordant identification). The patient projects self and objects into the therapist, and the therapist internalizes and identifies with some of these projections.

Question: What role does projective identification play in the negative therapeutic reaction?

Seinfeld: Projective identification is a concept originally defined by Melanie Klein and Wilfred Bion. In the earliest months of life, the infant suffers considerable anxiety over fear of annihilation and concerns that the power of its affect will overwhelm itself and the caregiver. The infant phantasyzes putting dangerous parts of itself into the caregiver. Klein believed that projective identification occurs only in phantasy whereas Bion expanded the concept by describing how the infant pressured the caregiver to experience and identify with the projection. Thus, Bion pointed out that projective identification was not only an intrapsychic but also an interpersonal event.

Bion described the maternal function as containing the child's anxieties and projections. Once the infant projects unwanted aspects of the self onto the caregiver, the infant experiences her as frightening. The infant then internalizes this frightening object to control it. The infant now experiences itself like this object it is identified with and attempts to project and get rid of this troublesome and alien part of itself. The good-enough actual mother accepts the infant's projections and anxieties but is able to metabolize them through a state of reverie and return to the infant a manageable, acceptable view of itself.

British object relations theory views projective identification not only as a defense but also as a preverbal mode of communication. The patient suffering preverbal trauma might attempt to communicate the nature of that trauma through projective identification. If the therapist feels unusually apathetic or bored with a particular patient, there might be a reenactment of early neglect and detachment. If the therapist feels unwanted or wants to be rid of the client, there could be a reliving of early abandonment and abuse. If the therapist feels unusually admiring of a client or is inclined to be admired, there may be a reenactment of early narcissistic issues. A male therapist seeing an adolescent female client felt uncomfortably aroused sexually. It was later learned that she was being sexually abused by her stepfather. The libidinally charged atmosphere in their relatedness was a communication about the abuse. The above examples point to the importance of the therapist being aware of, and acknowledging, countertransference responses. In the case of beginning therapists, it is essential that supervisors are open and accepting and create an atmosphere in which all countertransference responses are acceptable to share.

In response to the negative therapeutic reaction, the therapist might not only feel inadequate but even fear that he or she is malevolent or destructive because the patient is getting worse. These patients are especially demanding and difficult and may arouse considerable frustration and anger in the therapist and thereby exacerbate the therapist's guilt over the worsening conditions. As mentioned in chapter 1, projective identification can originate from the therapist as well as the patient, and the intensity of the patient's positive and negative transferences can be affected by the therapist's projections.

Question: What is meant by the holding relationship?

Seinfeld: Winnicott described the function of holding in the context of the caregiver's management of the space between mother and infant. Holding refers to how the caregiver enables the infant to tolerate separateness. The nature of holding changes in accordance with the child's developmental needs. Thus, in the beginning of life the caregiver experiences a state of primary maternal preoccupation in order to anticipate the baby's needs and its nonverbal cues. In one aspect of early holding, the caregiver serves as an environmental mother providing the secure condition of keeping the baby warm, dry, fed, and safe. It is hoped that the baby can securely forget the mother and simply "go on being." The caregiver offers herself as an object mother for the infant's needs, desire, love, hate, and interest. In this function, the object mother provides holding by surviving the infant's instinctive attacks without overstimulating or rejecting it.

In the course of development, the holding relationship gradually develops from a physical into a psychological relationship. As the baby relates to the mother over a greater physical distance, it discovers its environment. Winnicott stresses that much of the infant's environment is put there by the caregiver but that she must allow the infant the opportunity to discover it for himself to make it his own creation. It is very important for the infant's sense of creativity for it to have the experience of creating its world. In this space of separation, the infant discovers a favorite blanket, pillow, or teddy bear that in some subjective way has the smell, feel, or texture of the mother. Winnicott refers to the space of separation as potential or transitional space and the blanket or teddy bear as a transitional object. The infant knows the transitional object is not the mother, nor is it an internal object, but it reminds the infant of the mother and allows it the sense of control it wishes it had over the actual mother. The transitional object makes the space of separation tolerable by allowing the child to feel related to the mother while feeling the pain and longing of separation. Winnicott states that the experience with the transitional object is the foundation for the individual's later capacity to feel ego related when the person is alone.

Question: What is the clinician's holding function in working with the negative therapeutic reaction?

Seinfeld: The patient has a negative reaction to separating from bad objects because there is not yet a sufficient internal good object to replace them. Thus, the therapist must provide the patient with some transitional experiences to allow the emotional holding space of separation. For example, when the therapist goes away for vacation, if the patient is lacking in object constancy, it might be useful to drop the patient an innocuously worded note or postcard as a transitional object. In some instances, it might not be necessary to do something so concrete, and instead the therapist might explain how the patient's anger over the therapist's absence may cause the patient to withdraw emotionally and thereby obliterate the patient's image of the therapist. The clinician could suggest that the patient try to remain emotionally in contact with the therapist through his or her anger instead of withdrawal. When the patient is separating from bad objects, even the ordinary intervals between sessions might seen unbearable, and the therapist might have to allow for limited phone calls or make similar explanatory interventions.

Question: Is there a danger that such direct or concrete interventions will be overstimulating?

Seinfeld: Yes. It is important that the clinician listens to verbal and nonverbal cues as to how the client is reacting to such holding interventions. If these interventions are based on the therapist's and not the client's needs, the client will experience the clinician as an exciting object, which will in turn provoke an antilibidinal reaction. A patient was suicidal and too depressed to reach out to the therapist. The therapist agreed to call the patient to see how she felt during weekends when the clinic was closed. The therapist called the patient at appointed times, and on one occasion the patient was not there and later said that she felt better but forgot the appointed call. This was an indication that the patient no longer needed the therapist to call, and if the latter did so, the patient would have experienced him as overgratifying.

Question: What is the criteria for intervening with holding or interpreting?

Seinfeld: Generally, holding is an intervention that results in the building of psychic structure, holding transitional space, and helping the client internalize the therapist as a potentially good enough object. Therefore, holding is provided for what is lacking in psychic development and aims at promoting growth in whatever structures are lacking. Interpretation is aimed at the persistent ties to bad objects and serves to liberate the client from his or her bad objects. In object relations therapy with the negative therapeutic reaction, holding and interpreting are equally important interventions.

III

Intervention with the
Out of Contact Patient

Question: What is the out of contact phase?

Seinfeld: The phrase "out of contact" refers not only to the interpersonal behavior of the patient but also to the feeling of unrelatedness. The patient feels unrelated because there is not a secure enough relatedness to a good enough internal object. When alone, the individual does not feel lonely for others but rather isolated and hopeless.

Question: Wouldn't all patients experience some degree of an initial out of contact phase?

Seinfeld: Yes. It is natural for the client to become gradually engaged in the therapeutic process and to go through oscillating periods of relative relatedness and unrelatedness. For the patient inclined to merge with the therapist, experiences of unrelatedness may be the patient's way of beginning to separate.

Question: In that case, how do you distinguish the patient who is primarily out of contact?

Seinfeld: The patient who is primarily out of contact will enact withdrawal and flight from nearly all emotionally significant situations. The individual will be constantly "on the run" in the sense of continually changing jobs, relationships, living arrangements, career choices, friends, and so forth. If the person has a steady relationship, job, or living arrangement, he will remain noticeably emotionally aloof and distant. The individual is either radically uncommitted or uninvolved. This situation differs from the patient who is only on occasion out of contact and fears commitment but does become relatively involved in relationships, friendships, and home situations.

One out of contact patient who had been in treatment for two years spoke in a flat monotonous tone that dulled and bored the therapist. One day, the patient questioned the therapist if anything was wrong. The therapist asked why, and the patient said the therapist looked unusually sleepy and wondered if he was becoming ill. The therapist asked if he had ever looked sleepy before, and the patient replied no. In fact, the therapist had been as sleepy in previous sessions. Therefore, the patient's recognition of the therapist's drowsiness was an indication that the patient was becoming more related and aware of the therapist.

Some out of contact patients could be very talkative, but there is the sense that the patient is talking to himself and has no need for a response from the therapist.

Question: How does the out of contact patient experience himself?

Seinfeld: The out of contact patient experiences himself as going through life as an automaton. There is little sense of relatedness or autonomy. The patient suffers from derealization and depersonalization and experiences himself as going through the motions of living in a dulled, unreflective state. There is often the experience of a barrier between the individual and the world. One patient said he felt as if he were separated from the world around him by a plastic covering. The feeling of a protective shield prevented life from being too pleasurable or painful. He dreamt he was attacked by furious, large cats, but this covering prevented him from being ripped to pieces.

Question: How is the out of contact phase relevant to the negative therapeutic reaction?

Seinfeld: These patients suffer a structural deficit in the sense that they never had the opportunity to internalize a good enough object that could serve as a receptor for taking in the therapeutic relationship. These patients do not experience a sense of deprivation because they literally do not know what they are missing. As they begin to take in and accept the therapist's support and become aware of what they have missed, they may experience an awakening of longing. Because neither the therapist nor anyone can fulfill these early needs, the patient may be flooded with rage, setting in motion the negative therapeutic reaction.

Question: What is meant by the concept of structural deficit?

Seinfeld: Whereas bad objects are repressed and split off, good objects are conscious pleasurable memories that support and sustain the central self. If there is a lack of such good objects, ego functioning remains minimally developed. Frustration, tolerance, judgment, anticipation of consequences, affect regulation, and perception are all impaired. Interventions can address the structural deficit by showing these patients that they are lacking object constancy. The therapist initiates this process by empathetically demonstrating through the clinical material that the patient is not able to expect help from the therapist or to internalize potentially positive aspects of the therapeutic relationship.

The severely disturbed borderline patients' well-known sensitivity to environmental impingement is the result of the dominance of internal bad objects, which transforms a difficult problem into an utterly hopeless one. The patient's incapacity to use the therapist's potential help becomes the medium through which the therapist demonstrates the patient's lack of object constancy. It is important that the patient not experience the therapist's interventions as accusatory in the sense of blaming her for not making use of the therapy.

The following case discussion will focus on the clinical management of a patient's severe rejecting behavior in the transferential relationship. The patient suffered from severe environmental hardships. It will be demonstrated that the therapist can respond to the patient to facilitate the internalization of the therapist as a helping object. These interventions are particularly relevant during the out of contact and symbiotic phases of the transference evolution. The issue of countertransference is also important.

DIANE

Diane was a twenty-nine-year-old Latino woman seeking help for her latency age son, who was having academic and behavioral problems in school. She had also been reported to the child welfare authorities for child abuse and neglect before coming for help. I treated Diane for five years.

Diane's mother was Puerto Rican, and her father was Haitian. Diane grew up in a large family supported by public assistance. She and her siblings were severely abused by an embittered mother. Once, after Diane and her mother had quarreled, her mother beat her with a metal rod until she was covered with blood. Such incidents resulted in the temporary removal of Diane and her siblings from the home by child welfare authorities. Diane's father, an alcoholic, deserted the family during her childhood. Although Diane was of Puerto Rican and Haitian descent, she identified herself exclusively as Puerto Rican because her father had abandoned her.

Diane made a serious suicide attempt in adolescence and left home shortly thereafter. She began to live with a man, became pregnant, and left him when he asked her to marry him. She said she wanted no part of an emotional commitment.

Since that time, Diane lived with her son and worked sporadically at various jobs. She generally sought temporary positions where she could work her own hours and live independently. Unable to get along with supervisors or coworkers, she would quit or get fired. She moved a great deal and was evicted on occasion for not paying the rent.

Diane preferred to see only married men because they would not expect commitment. If a man became serious about their relationship, she would leave. She sought relationships in which she and the man clearly understood that they used each other for sex and for fun. During the time of treatment, she was seeing two men who were married. I often wondered how she survived the precariousness of her existence. She said everyone asks her that.

She saw herself as a survivor and explained that throughout her adolescence she went to the toughest schools in the Bronx and fought constantly to survive. She was so violent and disruptive that she was eventually placed in a junior high school for delinquent youth. Because of her reputation for violence, the other girls eventually left her alone. She did not belong to a street gang and wanted only to be left alone. Once this occurred, she did quite well academically because she was very bright.

The Problem of the Patient Acting Rather Than Reflecting

Diane began treatment on a once-weekly basis. She had been to the clinic about a year earlier and after a few sessions came in high on marijuana. She reported that the clinician had lectured her, so she walked out and did not return.

There was a hyperactivity about Diane. She would sit on the edge of her seat, as if she were ready to pounce, shifting about uncomfortably and continually looking at her watch. She did not stay for the full session but left after "saying her piece." Often the session lasted only for twenty minutes. She would discuss the events of the week—a fight with her current supervisor, a problem with her son, or a quarrel with her lover. She was extremely action oriented and described all situations in terms of the actions and behavior of the participants, without any reflection or insight into underlying feelings or motivations. She described a fight with a female supervisor.

"She stormed into the office. It was full of people, but she stood over me like the Incredible Hulk. She was a huge woman, large like a mountain. With her hands on her hips, towering over me, she shouted, 'Diane?' I just looked at her, and she raved at me like a mad woman, screaming that she can't stand me anymore, who do I think I am, and that I can't continue like this any more. The next thing I knew I was on my feet, too. We were screaming back and forth. I thought I'd hit her. I walked out. I put on my coat and said, 'Drop dead, you pig' and walked right out. If I return tomorrow and she says one word, I'll hit her. She's a big lady. I'm large, but she is a mountain. She might kill me. I'll stick her with my knife first."

A Lack of Communication between Patient and Therapist

During these initial sessions, it was impossible to get a sense of what was causing Diane's interpersonal problems. Diane would not reflect on why her supervisor hated her, on whether she had any part in the problem. If I asked her what she thought was happening between herself and the supervisor, she would present another action-filled story. After the telling, she wanted no feedback from me. It seemed that my role was to serve as a witness to her story. Given that her work and housing situations were unstable and that she tended to be depressed and hopeless between jobs, I felt a responsibility to confront her with the self-destructive quality of her actions. If I attempted, while empathizing with her feelings, to point out the self-destructive quality of her actions, she just stared at me as if I were a creature from another planet. If I said something to the effect that she spites herself when she walks off a job, she looked at me as if I were a fool. She could not verbalize her disagreements or lack of understanding, no matter how much I attempted to elicit such discussion. Instead, she communicated through movements or facial expressions.

When a problem arose in her life, such as unemployment or the threat of eviction, she was less eager to see me. She often did not come in or call to cancel. When she did appear and I opened the subject up for discussion, she would say it was a waste of time to talk about the situation, that she must act and do something about it. She would look at her watch as if the only problem she faced was sitting here and talking to me and that this oppressive discussion was the only thing getting in the way of her acting to solve her problem. No sooner would I think this than she would rise to leave. Interventions such as, "You are right. You do have to act to solve your problems, but sometimes sitting down and first figuring out the problem, getting some distance from it, could help you act more effectively," were met with a blank stare. I would ask if she agreed or had other thoughts, and she would shrug and roll her eyes as if to say, "I wish he'd shut up already so I could get out of here and do something useful."

Empathy was no more effective than problem solving, confrontation, or pointing out reality. For instance, as Diane described the hardships and struggles in her life, she would look at me if I expressed understanding, as if to say, "So what if you understand what good does that do for me?" If I made an empathic statement about how she feels that everyone is trying to control her, she looked as if she could not wait for me to be quiet so that she could either continue to talk or leave. When I commented that the abuse and oppression she experienced in her current life was similar to that which she suffered from earliest childhood, she looked at me as if to say, "So what else is new." If I interpreted that oppression and instability were all that she had ever known, so that she might be afraid of actively trying to change her life, to take control instead of passively suffering and fleeing from her troubles, she looked at me as if to say, "What is he talking about?"

I do not mean to suggest that every week, in frustration and exasperation, I tried a different approach. Rather, I tried those interventions over a four-year period and found most ineffectual. Yet she continued to come, though irregularly we did have one area of mutual understanding—that it was bad for her to beat up her child. Therefore, when she was angry with him, she no longer hit him but instead broke things or threw things around in her house. Once she was in a rage at him for watching television and not doing his homework. She refrained from beating his brains out and instead kicked in the television screen. Another time, she punched her fist through a window and needed to go to the hospital for treatment. When I encouraged her to verbalize instead of act on her angry feelings, she replied that she felt better when she threw something, broke something, or hit something. She said that she verbalized her angry feelings as well but that action made her feel better. Much of her communication to me was through facial expressions. On those rare occasions when she felt pleased with something I said, she would look directly at me and laugh. When she was angry, she would snarl. When she thought what I said was stupid, she would roll her eyes as if to say, "What is wrong with him?" At other times, she would stare at me blankly, as if I were communicating in a strange language.

Question: How does the clinician intervene with the action-oriented client?

Seinfeld: Diane's action orientation could be explained as a manic defense against underlying depression. There is a likely cultural component as well in that Diane's Latino heritage oftentimes values action as speaking louder than words. Psychotherapeutic technique reflects Anglo-European values in idealizing the word over action. Freud viewed repetition and acting out as a resistance to remembrance of things past and verbalization. Hence, the classical psychoanalytic technique is to have the patient "put everything into words" and to often interpret action as acting out. In working with persons from cultures that place greater value on action, it is important for the clinician to view action as a significant form of communication and not merely as acting out. Diane would often arrive late or miss appointments and present reasons, such as the bus did not arrive, the weather was problematic, her son was not feeling well, and so forth. When I suggested that she might be experiencing mixed feelings about therapy, she did not understand and insisted that if she did not want to come, she would quit. I eventually realized the importance of recognizing her actions as significant communications and explained that there was a split between her thoughts and her actions. Her thoughts were of sincerely wanting to come, but her feet told her another story. She let her feet do some of her talking by keeping her from coming. I reminded her of the phrase "action speaks louder than words," and the part of her that did not wish to come expressed itself not in thought but rather in action. I also explained that it is natural for an individual to have mixed feelings about coming for therapy, but Diane split those feelings into thoughts and actions and that we must listen not only to her thoughts but also to her actions. For a long time, I had been bewildered by Diane's behavior and did not make this intervention. I learned it was also important to ask her what she did instead of asking "why" or how she felt.

Question: What are some of the countertransference issues that arise in working with the action-oriented patient?

Seinfeld: As I listened to Diane over the first years of treatment, I noted two opposing tendencies in myself. Sometimes I attempted to understand her worldview. At other times, I wanted her to adapt to social reality and morality, to impose a higher developmental level and structure. She had a favorite expression she used when irritated. She would say, "I'm not going to entertain this anymore." On occasion, I found myself repeating this phrase in my own mind when I was irritated about something. At other times, I would be in an unpleasant situation and would imagine what Diane would have done in the same circumstance. I would picture her doing whatever she pleased without worrying about the consequences of reality or morality, and I would envy and admire her. In this way, I carried an image of her in my mind, and she became an internal object to me. I wondered whether my reality—morality interventions—were not the result of envy of her daring to do whatever she pleased. I now perceived the situations she discussed through her eyes. I became intrigued with how she experienced and felt about everything. This was not only an objective, scientific interest, although that too played a part, but also an intensely personal one in the sense that I felt there were important things that I could learn from her. This internal shift also marked a change in the actual treatment process.

For the first four years, Diane was inconsistent about keeping appointments. She would come for several weeks and then disappear for a time without calling. We might run into each other in the neighborhood. She would say, "I've been intending to call you." I would hear from her shortly afterward. At first when she disappeared, I would call her to find out what had happened. She would say that she had forgotten to make an appointment. After a while, I gave up on calling her. In this way, our relationship was detached. I first rationalized permitting her space by thinking that she needed distance because of her fear of engulfment, but now I wondered about my own fear of symbiosis. I also had the feeling that she was headed toward disaster, that she was a volcano ready to explode, and I was not interested in being close when it happened. She had always indicated that she felt people who pursued her were stupid, and I had some sense that she derived pleasure in making people stupid. I now wondered if her internal rejected object did not keep others, including me, at bay by making them feel stupid if they tried to establish a meaningful relationship with her.

41

A second problem occurred to me. Her constant crises were always the focus of our sessions. It felt absurd to focus on the therapeutic relationship when she had such pressing reality concerns. We discussed these concerns week after week, but nothing seemed to change. I felt that we were going around in circles, that her reality crisis stood between us, and that she did not have a significant enough internal relationship with me to use my help. Yet I felt this patient needed to work more in the transference to begin to cope with and change her environmental situation. I decided to address these issues with her.

Question: How does the therapist track the patient's absence of an internal object?

Seinfeld: The point of entry was her tendency to miss appointments. I did not approach this problem from the perspective of resistance or limit setting. Rather, I became intrigued with how she experienced or did not experience our relationship during these absences. I thought of myself as a professional helping person, and intellectually at least, she accepted this designation of my role. She realized she was in something called psychotherapy with me, and she came in and discussed problems in the role of a patient. On an emotional level, however, at least during certain periods, she did not seem to expect any help. I said this to her and added that when she disappeared, she did not have a picture in her mind of my being able to help. She explained that during times of severe stress, such as when she was short of money or threatened by unemployment or eviction,

> "The thought of you does not enter my mind. I completely forget that you, that even this office, exist."

I said, "Then you are all alone with your problems."

She replied, "I've been alone all my life. I always solved my problems alone."

I said, "Sometimes that has worked, but sometimes the problems seem too great for you to handle. They seem insurmountable, and since you feel all alone, you feel totally hopeless and helpless to manage them, so you give up and become depressed, and in giving up, there is no chance to change anything."

I asked what happened to her relationship with me in her mind between sessions. She looked at me, as if I were crazy, and said that she never thought of it. I asked if she ever thought about the therapy when faced with a problem. When she felt depressed or angry, did she ever reflect on what we had discussed?

"Never," she replied.

I said, "It is like I disappear for you when you leave."

She replied, "Yes, it's like that with everyone and everything. I forget that my own son exists. People get angry at me because I forget appointments or don't call them. I don't do it on purpose. It's always been like that. I never thought about it before." Laughing, she added, "It's not normal, is it?"

For the first time since I had been treating her, she looked curious as to how I would respond. I said, "It can be a problem. When you forget everyone, you are all alone inside."

She replied, "Sometimes I feel isolated, not lonely. I don't want other people's company. I like being alone. But sometimes I feel that there is no place for me, like I'm an outcast.

43

I never fit in anywhere. I don't fit in with my family. I didn't fit in with other kids, and I can't fit in on a job. I always feel misplaced."

Now when she failed to come for appointments, I called her five minutes into the session. I told her I was doing so to help her remember the therapeutic relationship. She would say she had forgotten. Then she would run to the clinic, which was a few blocks from her apartment. She now said, "I'm crazy, but I never know exactly how. Now I'm starting to see. Not everyone forgets people like I do. But I don't know what to do about it. It just happens automatically."

Question: What are some of the psychological and cultural factors contributing to the patient's forgetting of appointed times?

Seinfeld: As Lunch and Hanson point out, different cultures have varying relationships to time. In Latino culture, the sense of time is organic and measured by however long it takes to complete a task or solve a problem. People's lives are not so much lived by the clock. One visits another when in need and not because it is the appointed time. In Anglo-American culture, people's lives are much more determined by the clock. Such phrases as "time is money" or "it is a waste of time" reflect the cultural sense that time is a valuable commodity that can be well or frivolously spent. The psychotherapeutic culture of the fixed hour clashed with Diane's sense that the therapy should occur when she felt the need.

In the classic analytic tradition, a patient's keeping or forgetting appointments, according to the need or lack thereof, would be understood as an indication of primitive need satisfying level of object relations. It is as if the therapist ceases to exist in the patient's mind when the patient no longer needs him. The clinician would hold firmly to the analytic frame and interpret the patient's aroused oral rage over frustration. When the patient's difficulty in adapting to the therapeutic frame has to do with a different cultural relationship to time, it is important for the clinician to become more flexible and, where possible, to adapt the frame to the patient and not expect the patient do all the adapting. Therefore, while treating Diane, I sometimes called her when she did not arrive and was flexible in scheduling and rescheduling appointments. If the therapist's schedule does not permit a flexible frame, it is essential to acknowledge that the therapeutic structure might seem rigid and strange to the patient.

Diane's difficulty in adapting to the frame had to do not only with cultural factors but also with the lack of object constancy. She acknowledged that forgetting her son and significant others was the result of feeling unrelated and isolated. Therefore, it was necessary for the therapy to focus on developing object constancy.

Question: How does the therapist enable the patient to develop greater psychic structure?

Seinfeld: In the event of psychic conflict, the clinician intervenes by interpreting and uncovering. When faced with a structural deficit, the clinician helps the patient become aware of the lack or deficiency in psychic structure and functioning. The patient cannot be expected to initiate a new area of psychic functioning until she becomes aware of what is missing.

Over the next three months, there were some subtle indications that Diane was internalizing me. The first sign occurred when she called me at the exact moment our session was to begin and said, "Do we have an appointment today? I'm not sure." She began to show some beginning capacity to expect help by saying that she wanted to see me first thing in the morning, before starting her job hunt or going to work on a temporary job, to get herself going. She noticed that the workers in the clinic were drinking coffee, so she asked me if she could have some to clear her head during our early appointments. On the one hand, it might be thought that she did not expect much feeding from me, so she wanted to feed herself concretely in order to avoid her oral rage at the depriving object. From this view, the coffee could serve to split off the negative transference. On one level, I believe this interpretation is accurate but incomplete. Splitting can also serve internalization for a time by allowing the patient to begin to internalize an all-good object. By asking for coffee, she was beginning to take something in from me and internalize a positive image of the object as feeding her. She initially gulped down the coffee. The atmosphere of the sessions changed radically. She stopped sitting at the edge of her seat and glancing at her watch. She pulled over another chair, lifted her feet on it, and semireclined. I did the same.

She alternated between remembering and forgetting our appointments. I noticed that whenever we had a particularly good session and I felt close to her, she would forget the following one. I did not interpret her rejection of closeness or involvement but remained focused on her inability to remember our relationship. Thus, I focused on helping her recognize the structural deficit as opposed to interpreting her conflicts about closeness/distance. She became more aware that she did not keep in her mind positive experiences with others. She began to wonder aloud why she had this "lack," as she called it. I made a very general statement that "when a person has not had many positive experiences with others, they grow up not being able to recognize or take in such experience. It is as if they do not recognize help or care when they see it. It is like something from another planet." I made it clear that it was not her fault. She could not take in or hold on to something she never had. I also posed a problem to her. "Therapy is supposed to be about providing something tangible, something that you can't see. If you are out of a job, in danger of eviction, or broke, I don't pull a job, money, or apartment out of a hat. I might inform you where you might get what you need and even help you find a community resource, but I myself don't provide you with material help. Instead, therapy is about providing emotional help and you taking in that help and you and I studying our relationship. But this is all very vague and mystical sounding to you—you have not had the life experience to even know what such help is, so our first step together is to learn about that."

She replied, "I don't have the faintest idea about what emotional help or emotional connection or relationships mean. I know of people who go to therapists and say they feel much better, supported, and helped in their lives. I don't know about emotion in that way. I just can't do it."

Question: How does the clinician enable the patient to develop self-empathy?

Seinfeld: A basis had now been established for encouraging Diane to explore childhood memories in order to understand how she never had opportunities for the establishment of meaningful object relations. She recalled that as a young child, she had saved all her pennies to fix her shoes when they wore out. She could not ask her parents to fix her worn shoes. Not only would they refuse, but they would blame her for not taking care of them

47

and severely beat her. She now told me about the time her mother calculatedly attacked her with a metal rod.

As she recalled numerous experiences of abuse and neglect, she said that she had never thought of these horrendous experiences as strange, unusual, or in any way abnormal. Her thought had only carried her to the conclusion that she was a bad kid and that her parents hated her for it, so she in turn hated them. But she thought this is the way it was and always would be, and she would therefore have to go it alone and not be bothered with people. She could not remember any occasions of making up with a parent after a fight or about their inquiring about any of her activities. She did recall that if she spoke her own opinion about a family problem, she was beaten. As she recalled these incidents, she felt flooded with rage and wanted to put a knife through her mother. She said that at a very early age, she decided that she would hate everyone around her and go it alone and take care of herself.

For the first time since I had known her, she became decidedly discontent with her life situation. She said she had no direction, that she was turning around in circles. Before, when she became hopeless and depressed when she was out of work, she would grit her teeth, tell herself she had to get tough, and find some temporary answer to her problem. She said, "I never before questioned my own life, only some uncomfortable part of it." She began to want more for herself, a steady place to live, a regular job, and reliable friends, but she had no idea how to effect it. She said, "I'm beginning to feel that I've spent my entire life just existing, seeing only the surface, acting blindly merely to survive. It's like I'm becoming aware and everything is collapsing." She began to feel vulnerable about her life situation and empathized with herself for the mess her life was in and the opportunities she never had.

Question: How does the patient begin to feel empathy for the parents and some of the cultural and societal factors impacting them?

Seinfeld: One day, Diane noticed a book her son had brought home from school. It was Richard Wright's autobiography *Black Boy*. She became engrossed. She explained that it was a black family exploited and abused in the white majority society of the Deep South. The author described how the parents vented their frustration and powerlessness by viciously abusing him. It was dangerous for a black boy to grow up with ambitions, competitiveness, and a striving for success and autonomy. Numerous stories were told at home of blacks who were lynched by hostile and envious whites for "not knowing their place." The parents would viscously beat him if he asserted his own opinion, disrespected his elders, and disregarded his place. If he behaved with confidence, it was beaten out of him. In this way, they tried to prepare him for a hostile, dangerous world. Diane found her own experience of abuse in childhood to be quite similar to what Wright described. She was enraged at her current situation and lack of opportunities. Yet she also felt empathic for her parents, who were victims as well.

Diane described writing a résumé for seeking a job but then imagining an employer ridiculing the résumé and throwing it away. She then threw her nearly completed résumé into the wastebasket. I remarked that she herself was the boss who rejected her own effort to find work. She recalled that her mother had thrown away her letter of acceptance into college. The university did contact her, and she went but felt invisible and neglected and eventually dropped out. It was shortly after this occasion that she finally left her mother's home permanently. She was among the first Latino students accepted into this college with a scholarship. The university was comprised mostly of Caucasian upper-middle-class students and faculty. She now realized that her mother must have felt frightened about the threat of losing her to another cultural world. The mother feared Diane would be lost to herself and her mother by going to live with people of a different culture, race, and social class. Diane internalized the mother's fear, but there was also reality to the mother's concern in that Diane was exposed to a form of racism and prejudice in that she was often ignored and neglected. Because the racism was not overt but rather covert, she could not even get angry but instead increasingly withdrawn. She was now able to experience ambivalence toward her mother because she realized that her mother not only held her back but was also frightened for her, and she was able to work on her anger at the people in college for not providing her with support.

Question: Is the cognitive-psychological belief that depressive patients view the world through a cognitive scheme of negativity relevant in object relations therapy?

Seinfeld: Yes. Depressive patients perceive their environment from the cognitive-affective schema of something lacking—the glass-half-empty syndrome. It could also be said that nondepressive individuals see the world through the cognitive-affective schema of idealization—the glass-half-full schema. The depressed patient's perception that something is lacking is not necessarily entirely false. The issue is that the patient focuses only on what is lacking or negative and does not focus on potential resources or sources of support and therefore feels hopeless since the patient constantly focuses on what she is deprived of. The therapist sees only the negative aspects of the patient's life and often becomes as hopeless as the patient.

From an object relations point of view, the negative cognitive-affective schema is based on the dominance of an internal depriving object. The client selectively perceives the depriving aspects of her life because her perception is entirely colored by the internal depriving object.

Question: What are the implications for intervention? Does the clinician focus on the client's negative worldview as a distortion and attempt to foster a more positive worldview?

Seinfeld: No. The client's perception of depriving or rejecting aspects of the world is not entirely a distortion, and the client's depressive reaction is not entirely illegitimate. If the therapist attempts to transform the negative into a positive outlook, the therapist will be artificially attempting to create a manic defense. Rather, the therapist should acknowledge and empathize with the depressing-depriving aspects of the client's life but then also point out that the client exclusively focuses on what is negative and thereby does not recognize or make use of potential sources of support. The therapist should enable the client to achieve a balance between what are the negative and positive polarities. Many clients suffer depressing life circumstances, and the recognition of this reality may enable some to mobilize the aggression necessary to try to change these life circumstances. The client's depressive reaction may be natural to the situation, so that the therapist should not attempt to deny this reality but instead help the client become better able to tolerate the depressive reaction without becoming hopeless. There are also clients who need to relive the early abandonment depression to become aware of their early rage at objects.

When Diane became hopelessly depressed and said there are no jobs out there, the therapist acknowledged that the job

51

situation was depressing but then said that her feeling of hopelessness, the belief that there was nothing whatsoever out there to help, was based on seeing the world through her early experiences of extreme deprivation.

Question: How does the therapist intervene with the manic defense?

Seinfeld: Diane needed to find a job by a certain deadline. She had agreed with her landlord in a court hearing to move out by a certain date to avoid immediate eviction. I realized she herself had brought this situation to a head, insisting it was time for her to face reality. She experienced her environmental crisis as a do-or-die situation. On the one hand, she faced "disaster, suicide, homelessness," and on the other hand, she faced "a new beginning, a new life, a chance for rebirth."

She would say she must face the necessity of finding a permanent job with a planned schedule where she could consistently keep her therapy appointments. Then she would cancel her appointment, saying she started a temporary job and had no time to come in. When the temporary job ended, she would come in and insist that the situation was hopeless, that she might as well be dead. I insisted that the situation was not hopeless. I said it was depressing but not hopeless unless she gave it up as hopeless. I said that when she felt hopeless, she was all alone in her mind again, she had lost her relationship to me and everyone else, and she again felt like a child carrying too great a burden. She then did not feel like giving up but felt depressed and angry. She then realized she had other work experience in the past she had not been remembering.

When she found a job, Diane was quite ambivalent. The thought of working nine to five, of sitting in an office all day, and of having to take orders felt overburdening, imprisoning. When she started, she sounded so depressed that I thought she would not last through the first week. She had to force herself to go in every day. She said, "You have no idea how terrible it is. I feel smothered. All these people in one office. I don't know how long I can take it. I feel like running out."

She decided to straighten out her own life. She had to endure it no matter what. She complained that her coworkers tried to socialize with her, talked about their family lives, tried to show pictures of their families, and asked her to join the group part of it. When someone tried to show her family pictures, she replied that she was there to work, not look at pictures. She described how she lost other jobs not because her work was poor but because she did not fit in with the people. She did not want to lose this job, but she could not pretend that she fit in with the people there. She mimicked how everyone said good morning to one another even though they hated being there. "Good morning, good morning, good morning, good morning," said as if she were an automaton. I asked how she replied to all the good mornings. She said she looked away, if possible, pretending not to hear. I said she did not feel like saying good morning. She felt like replying, "Fuck you."

She laughed and said that is right. She said, "Could you imagine the expression on their faces if I replied, 'Fuck you'?" I suggested that the next time one says good morning, she should think "fuck you" but say "good morning." I asked if she could do that. She laughed and said it is the best suggestion I ever made. I said that this might help her with her problem of trying to be sociable while not feeling like a hypocrite. She agreed it would be difficult to continue working at this job if she could not even say good morning to people. The next time we met, she said she tried what I had suggested—"Fuck you, good morning, fuck you, good morning—it was easier, much easier."

53

Question: How did the patient manifest her identification with the bad object and rejection of the therapist as a potential good object?

Seinfeld: Diane continued to feel stressed. Although she was employed, she still did not have enough money to move as the deadline approached. One day in April, Diane came into my office, sat down, and said, "I can't take it anymore." She took off her sunglasses and threw them against the wall, barely missing the window. Then she threw and broke an ashtray, screaming, "I can't take it. There's too much stress in my life. I don't want to be here today." I said, "Don't leave, stay . . ." she stormed out.

Later, I called her. She said, "I'm sorry I wrecked your office."

She then told me she had a fight with her son. She recited everything bad about him. She said he answered her back. She said he needed a fist in his face. She said all he understands is macho. "Well, I'm macho mom. I'll punch him in the face."

She told me she had packed his bags to send him to Puerto Rico, that she was giving up. She said she had sent him out to sell his cat. He could not take it with him. I said, "You always say that our sessions help, that you come in stressed and leave calm. Why did you storm out today? Why did you reject help just when you most need it? Instead of trying to take in help, you threw me out of your mind in throwing everything around. This is what you told me your mother always did. You needed something from her, and she went crazy and threw things."

She replied, "I couldn't help it. Today is one of the worst days of my life. I felt this way only once before, when I tried to kill myself after fighting with my mother. I'm not going to do that now. I'm worried about my son. This is too abrupt. I came home from you and told him I'm sending him away. He doesn't know what's going on. I'm going out to find him. He went to sell his cat. I'm going to find him first. He loves his cat."

In our next session, Diane was calmer and reflective. She had been out of control, on the edge and hopeless. My statements helped her feel back in control. She realized she had come to my office to reject my help. When I help her get in control, she feels controlled by me. She is not used to having someone influencing her. It felt strange, uncomfortable. She needed time to get used to it. When she remembered our relationship, she no longer felt hopeless. She could think straight. When she forgot me, she felt isolated and hopeless. She felt like a building that had been erected on a weak foundation; sooner or later, the foundation would collapse. She felt isolated, directionless. She felt she had no place in society, no contact point with it. A lot of it she said was outlook. When she was not hopeless, she could mobilize and plan ahead. When she was all alone inside, she felt out of contact with everything and believed there was no future for her.

In late spring, Diane came up with an idea to raise money just as the deadline approached. A former lover had given her a very expensive piece of furniture. She realized that it looked very out of place in her apartment and that since she no longer felt a need for it, she could sell it. She sold it for a thousand dollars, which enabled her to find an apartment. Although the furniture was there all along, she never before thought of selling it. The piece had become part of the woodwork, and she nearly forgot it was there. She attributed her discovery of it to a changed attitude.

IV

Manifestations of the Negative Therapeutic Reaction

Question: Are there stages in the treatment process that describe the negative therapeutic reaction?

Seinfeld: Searles (1967) described four phases of patient-therapist interaction in intensive psychotherapy of the severely disturbed patient. These phases can also be understood as a framework for understanding the various manifestations of the negative therapeutic reaction. They not only describe the sequential phases of patient-therapist interaction during the treatment process but also reflect early levels of object relations enacted in the transference-countertransference situation. Each specific phase of patient-therapist interaction also refers to the patient's developmental level of object relations and clinical diagnosis. The phases of patient-therapist interaction are (1) out of contact, (2) ambivalent (pathological) symbiosis, (3) therapeutic symbiosis, and (4) resolution of the symbiosis.

Question: What is the out of contact phase?

Seinfeld: In this phase, the patient and therapist are isolated in their own psychic territories until the patient gradually permits the therapist entry into his or her own psychic space. The therapist must avoid imposing his or her own internal world on the patient and tolerate the patient's distance. As Winnicott (1958) states, the therapist communicates an empathic under-standing of the patient's need for protection from impingement, and the patient begins to trust the therapist enough to allow for entry of the latter into the patient's world.

The out of contact patient does not know how to relate to the therapist as a potential good object. Lacking in good enough object relations experience that can serve as a receptor for internalizing the therapist as an empathic object, the patient experiences the therapist as an alien creature from another planet. Because of an incapacity to expect help from human object relations, the patient is for the most part indifferent to the therapist. These severely disturbed patients are described as experiencing a structural deficit in positive self and object representations. This deficit is, of course, not absolute, or the patient would never come for treatment. Many of these patients are referred or pressured into treatment from outside sources, but it can be assumed from the patient's continued attendance that there is a wish for help. When faced with a crisis or problem in their lives, those patients may become indifferent to the therapy and cancel or forget appointments. As one patient said, "When a serious problem arises, I never think of you. I forget that you exist, even that the building you work in exists. I must do something about the problem. Time to act. Sitting and talking is a waste of time, preventing me from doing whatever I need to do to take care of business."

Question: How does the out of contact patient experience self and other?

Seinfeld: The patient does not experience him- or herself as the author of his thoughts, feelings, or experiences; rather, these phenomena somehow happen to him. The patient is not the subject but rather the object of life. Those patients are unable to reflect on themselves or others. The dialectical process between fantasy and reality is broken down. The patient lives in a psychic world of concrete reality in which imagination is foreclosed (Ogden, 1986).

These patients are disconnected from human object relations and prefer relating to the nonhuman world. McDougall (1980) described them as antianalysands because they go through the motions of treatment but remain unaffected by the therapist's empathy and interpretations. They resemble the classic schizoid patient in the sense that they are concrete and reality bound; however, they are more impulsive and do not use the defense of isolation of affect. They often become disappointed and enraged in their object relations.

The out of contact patient will describe life events as stories that have happened to her. If the therapist explores the motivations of the patient or other people, the patient will usually tell another story. The patient experiences a strong sense of inevitability about any problem that arises and how the patient must react. If the patient were to reflect on him- or herself when faced with crises, it is likely that he or she would feel overwhelmed by a sense of vulnerability. The patient forecloses this possibility by reacting immediately to the problem.

A patient reported that she had finally begun to develop a subjective sense of self after many years of intensive psychotherapy. "It's as if all of my life I reacted automatically to anything that happened—just existing and reacting on automatic. I took the first answer at hand, never thinking about the long term or how my solution of today would sit in six months. I just reacted to the crisis. It was easier then. I didn't realize how difficult anything was. Consequences didn't occur to me. I didn't think about anything." For this patient, silent attacks on the capacity to think resulted in the dissociation of the vulnerable self.

The out of contact patient's discourse resembles the narration in a Kafka novel where the character is faced with a senseless, absurd, and meaningless reality that inevitably crushes him. The patient experiences himself as facing a world populated by shallow people who fulfill their pragmatic roles and functions to the point of meaningless absurdity; the patient experiences himself and people around him as abstractions who could be just as easily distinguished by initials. The patient compensates for his dreary, emotionally lifeless existence by attachments to exciting nonhuman objects. Drugs, alcohol, food, money, clothing, or nearly any nonhuman object can serve as the focus of an addiction compulsion to compensate for the lack of a human holding object. The insatiable need for things, in turn, generates crisis around such things enslaving the patient in an inevitable vicious cycle of crisis, need, and reaction.

Question: How does the out of contact patient manifest the negative therapeutic reaction in the transference-countertransference situation?

Seinfeld: The patient's reality, behavior, and crisis-bound life becomes the negative therapeutic reaction that closes the therapist out of the internal psychic system. The patient constructs a real crisis, in the context of which the therapist is useless, impotent, and ineffectual. It is important to note that the crises are real and not merely imaginary; however, the patient has constructed her reality in accord with her internal object world. This particular view, which has been an important development in contemporary object relations theory—that of mental construction of reality and the interpenetration of the patient's internal world and the environment—will inform most of the clinical vignettes of this book. This view does not presuppose that the internal world is more important than the external world; rather, it focuses on a complex interpenetration of internal and external worlds through projective and introjective identification.

The out of contact patient is unable to project a hoped-for good object into the therapist. These patients have given up hope for a rapprochement, reparation, or resurrection of the internal good enough object, usually because of extreme early abuse and/or neglect. They bring to mind T. S. Eliot's line from "The Wasteland" when he speaks of rats' alley and dead men who have lost their bones. Rats' alley refers to the internal psychic world, a waste land in which the internal bad object, the orally destructive rat, has even devoured and chewed the bones of the internal good object, leaving no hope for resurrection, rapprochement, or reparation.

If the patient is not undergoing a crisis, a therapeutic relationship is likely to be permeated with a sense of apathy reflecting the apathetic, futile climate of the patient's early object relations. When the patient is in the midst of crisis, the therapeutic relationship will be characterized by a sense of overwhelming despair and hopelessness. The patient is only able to perceive and describe the negative aspects of her life situation. The therapist is therefore unaware of any potentially helpful resources or good objects in the patient's life that could provide a counterbalance to the overwhelming problems. If the patient begins to internalize the therapist as a good object, then the crisis-need-reaction cycle becomes intensified in the negative therapeutic reaction in order to eject the therapist as useless and impotent. The active rejection of the therapist as a potential good object brings about the shift from the out of contact phase to ambivalent symbiosis.

Question: How is the ambivalent symbiosis manifested in the treatment relationship?

Seinfeld: Searles (1961) states that this phase has the feeling tone of sexuality and aggression, and patient and therapist often feel that they drive each other crazy. Once a break is established in the closed psychic system of the out of contact phase, the patient will experience the classic borderline rapprochement transference of rapid oscillations between clinging and distancing. Searles (1961) refers to this rapprochement merry-go-round as ambivalent symbiosis. The use of the term *symbiosis* implies a regression not to the symbiotic phase of total fusion between self and object but rather to the extensive use of projective identification (Grotstein, 1985). Mahler (1975) describes this phenomenon when she speaks of the rapprochement child who wants to separate from the mother and then projectively identifies this wish into her.

Question: What are the dynamics underlying the ambivalent symbiosis?

Seinfeld: The patient who has reached the phase of ambivalent symbiosis has a strong enough internal good object to project it into the transference. The internal bad object situation aborts the hoped-for good object by constructing an insatiable need for the good object. The potential good object thus invariably becomes an exciting and then a rejecting object. The self-component feeling rejected will then reject the exciting object. The sense of rejection then leads to depression associated with object loss, resulting in the recurrence of the wish to merge with the hoped-for good object and thereby again setting in motion the vicious cycle.

Question: What is the hoped-for good object?

Seinfeld: The hoped-for good object could be likened to the myth of the hero. Campbell (1949) discusses themes that recur throughout the myths of humankind related to the search of the hero for a reunion with a lost good object. In the reunion adventure, the hero repeatedly encounters gods, goddesses, demons, and witches who attempt to impede his journey toward reunion. Homer's Odyssey is a typical reunion adventure of this kind. Odysseus is separated from son, Telemachus, and wife, Penelope, by the Trojan War. The epic poem recounts his journey home and the demons, witches, and temptresses he must cunningly outwit in order to reunite with his wife and son. James Joyce, in his novel *Ulysses*, updates and relocates the Odyssey adventure to prewar Dublin. The hero, Bloom (symbolizing Odysseus as the father-husband), seeks reunion with his wife, Molly, and the symbolized son, Daedalus. The union is thwarted not by supernatural demons, witches, and temptresses but by ordinary characters in everyday Dublin who are perceived as similar to Homer's demons and witches in the narrator's stream of consciousness. Therefore, in the Joyce novel, they are depicted as the narrator's internal bad objects which impede the reunion with the hoped-for good object. The theme centering around the thwarting of the reunion with the hoped-for good object by bad internal objects is the basic dynamic of the negative therapeutic reaction during ambivalent symbiosis. The epic myth is reenacted in the transference-countertransference situation as the hoped-for reunion with the good object becomes activated in the transference, and the bad internal object world seeks to thwart the reunion.

In ambivalent symbiosis, the patient clings to the therapist in dependence. The clinging leads to a fear of loss of autonomy so the patient then distances with aggression. Clinging and distancing reflect the transformation of the hoped-for good object into an exciting, then rejecting, then rejected object. The therapist can eventually serve as a bridge in the integration of the split-off good and bad selves and objects. During this phase, the negative self and object components dominate over the positive components, reflecting the fact that the patient's internalized experience has been more bad than good. Thus, the splitting is indicative of the patient's effort to protect the fragile good object from being consumed by the dominant bad object. Antidependent resistance also continues to view the need for the hoped-for good object as a threat to fragile autonomy and must therefore reject the positive image of the therapist by transforming it into an exciting object. The patient's infantile unmet dependency needs are so great and insatiable that it is inevitable that the exciting object will be transformed into its rejecting counterpart. This ambivalent symbiosis phase is also characterized by the patient's putting third parties between herself and the therapist to create distance. Therefore, in the transference, the patient might become jealous and obsessed with the therapist's involvement with other objects, or she might preoccupy herself with other objects. The negative aspect of the ambivalent symbiotic phase is so intense as to threaten the therapeutic relationship with absolute disruption. Because of this threat of object loss, the positive aspect of the symbiosis becomes dominant, resulting in the phase of the therapeutic symbiosis.

Question: According to ego psychology, symbiosis is considered to be pathological beyond infancy. Therefore, how can a symbiotic phase in the transference be considered therapeutic?

Seinfeld: The notion that symbiotic experience must come to a radical halt after the first months of life may be an expression of the Anglo-American bias of valuing individualism over relatedness. I would suggest that the Mahlerian stages of symbiosis and separation-individuation be considered not as static hard and sequential periods that must begin and end in a definitive period but rather as modes of organizing experience—developmental positions in the British object relations sense—that occur in developmental sequence but may recur in later periods. There are natural symbiotic experiences throughout the life cycle—experiencing a sense of oneness and communion with nature, making love and falling in love, mystical experience, and so forth. Symbiotic experience is to be considered pathological if one's relationship or relationships were for the most part symbiotic. However, one could have the capacity for symbiotic experience in the context of having achieved a relatively strong degree of autonomy. Similarly, the practicing position could occur at different times in the life cycle and be associated with the sense of elation over adventure, novelty, and facing the unknown. Rapprochement would be associated with the sense of vulnerability that is a natural occurrence in response to the changes that occur throughout the life cycle. Differentiation would recur in relation to those experiences in which one reasserts one's identify. The sense of who one is and who one is not, awakening to one's sense of cultural, racial, or gender or ethnic identity, would be affirmative experiences in differentiation as well as group solidarity.

Borderline patients who have not had a positive symbiotic experience in early life that provided a foundation for relatedness and autonomy will need to experience symbiotic relatedness with a therapist to feel secure enough to risk individuation. This symbiotic relatedness is not an actual regression to the psychic state of symbiosis in the first months of life. It is rather a playing at symbiosis in transition space (Winnicott, 1971).

The dilemma is that the borderline patient experiences transference as real and not as illusion and therefore will relive early experience as if it is occurring in the here and now. Thus, moments of closeness and caring in the therapeutic relationship will be experienced as idyllic and blissful, and separations and disruptions will be experienced as traumatic and as if the patient has only the psychic resources of an infant to manage the distress.

Question: What is the feeling tone of the therapeutic symbiosis?

Seinfeld: Searles (1961) states that the feeling tone of therapeutic symbiosis is one of maternal care and love, with the receding of sexual and aggressive trends. In the phase of symbiosis, there is full reemergence of the vulnerable and fearful regressive, dependent self in the care and protection of the idealized, holding therapist. The patient and therapist can sometimes interchange transferential positions, according to Searles (1961). The patient assumes the role of the omnipotent mothering object, and the therapist assumes the role of the vulnerable child. During this phase, the feeling tone between patient and therapist is akin to "you and me against the world," also suggesting that the bad internal object situation is projected into the external world that "you and me" are against. Searles (1961) has remarked on the great difficulty in distinguishing whether the manifestations of the therapeutic symbiosis are a truly preambivalent relatedness or a folie à deux between the participants that splits off and denies aggression between them. Possibly it is not an either-or situation but rather one in which symbiosis is therapeu-

66

tic in terms of allowing the patient an opportunity to internalize a positive self and object representation but a folie à deux in terms of denying and splitting off aggression. I see this folie à deux aspect not in pejorative terms but in the context of what I described earlier as the therapeutic symbiosis being a form of play occurring in the transitional psychic space (Winnicott, 1971).

The therapeutic symbiosis marks the gradual integration of the active oral and passive vulnerable split-off dependent self. The vulnerable self becomes increasingly less withdrawn and passive as it actively asserts the need for the holding object. The patient can thereby begin to integrate the good holding object and bad exciting object. In his experience of the dependent transference, Winnicott (1960) describes how the therapist gradually becomes more of a holding object for ego care and less of an object for gratification of instinctual needs. He says the patient's primary need for ego care gains ascendance over instinctual need gratification.

Winnicott (1960) says that regression in the transference permits emergence of and contact with the true self by the holding object therapist. Winnicott speaks of two aspects of the true self: the true self as fragile, vulnerable to internal and external impingement, and the true self as spontaneous, omnipotent and alive. These two aspects of the true self engage in two manifestations of the transference. The true self as vulnerable to impingement activates an omnipotent holding object transference. Kohut (1971) refers to this phenomenon as the idealizing self-object transference. The second aspect is that the true self in omnipotence seeks with a spontaneous gesture the gesture of acceptance by the holding object. He refers to this phenomenon as the mirroring self-object transference.

Question: What facilitates the emergence of the therapeutic symbiotic transference?

Seinfeld: The true self, which is analogous to the passive, withdrawn, regressed self (Guntrip, 1969), has become disconnected from the holding object because of traumatic failures in empathy and holding and because of antidependent bad object attacks against vulnerability, fear, and dependence. Winnicott says the true self is on ice, in cold storage, withdrawn and buried beneath the conflicts of active, oral, sadomasochistic, infantile dependence (ambivalent symbiosis). In disconnection with the holding object, the true self remains weak and vulnerable. The true self is in need of a holding object to thrive. Empathic communication with the true self's need to withdraw for protection paradoxically facilitates the emergence of the true self in the therapeutic symbiosis.

Question: What are the clinical problems associated with the therapeutic symbiosis?

Seinfeld: During this phase of treatment, the emerging true self is highly vulnerable to impingements of all sorts and to failures of empathy on the part of the therapist. The patient projects all goodness onto the therapist and is therefore highly susceptible to disappointment. The patient is now fully immersed in testing if the therapist is a good enough object providing a safe enough climate in which the patient can release his bad objects. The patient is now increasingly able to maintain a positive image of the therapist to comfort himself.

As the patient internalizes the therapist, he gradually becomes less dependent on the therapist and other objects. The patient may become both comforter and comforted. In unconscious phantasy, he becomes the internal good breast object. In becoming his own good object, the patient has achieved a narcissistic adaptation in which he denies his dependence and envy on the external good object. In this way, the narcissistic symbiotic phantasy that one contains the good object inside oneself results in the denial of dependence on separate, external objects. The continued presence of the therapist enables the patient to protect himself from the persecutory bad object. At first, he needs the actual contact with the therapist to reinforce and strengthen the internal good object.

The patient's external objects reinforce the phantasy that he is the good breast, and the needy self is sometimes projected onto the external object. The patient plays at the phantasy that he is the good object rescuing the weak, fragile self from the bad object. In order to psychically play the role of the good object, the patient must have had enough good early object relations experience in order to have a strong enough internal positive object representation to serve as a basis for psychic play. If the patient lacks such good enough early experience, the patient has the opportunity to internalize supportive and containing experience during the out of contact and ambivalent symbiotic phases. The phantasy that the patient has incorporated the good breast is manifest in the patient psychically playing at comforting and nurturing himself and thereby establishing a basis for resolving the symbiosis.

Question: How does the resolution of symbiosis occur?

Seinfeld: The resolution of the symbiosis is not the tail end of the treatment process but is of prolonged duration, sometimes longer than the combined previous phases. Searles (1961) says that the feeling tone of this phase is one of increasing conflict between symbiosis and separation individuation.

The emergence of aggression is now of central importance in that aggression serves separation individuation. Jacobson (1964) states that the splitting of all-good and all-bad self and object representations gradually gives way to the child's increasingly investing all badness in the object representation and all goodness into the self representation. The libidinal investment in the all-good self endows it with narcissism, ego interests, ambitions, and ideals. The aggression invested in the object serves autonomy and separation. From my own clinical experience, I believe that this all-good self/all-bad object appears in the disillusionment that occurs in the transference. As I described in the previous section, the patient takes a good part of his idealization into himself. He thereby begins to idealize his own ego interests and values. The internal bad object is then projected into the therapist. The patient now experiences a full-blown negative therapeutic reaction.

In the resolution of the symbiosis, the patient discovers the bad object in the transference by perceiving the therapist as engulfing, frightened of losing the patient, rejecting of autonomy, and jealous of the patient's other interests, relationships, and activities. The patient attempts to create the therapist as bad object through projective identification, and the therapist may, more or less unknowingly, enact the role of bad object in the countertransference. The patient now works at actively separating from the bad object that is jealous and fearful of losing him. The phase of the resolution of symbiosis is relevant to Searles's view that the patient becomes the analyst to the analyst. Fairbairn (1943) stated that the patient will release his repressed internal bad objects only if the therapist can be a good enough object in reality. However, it must also be remembered that the patient denies dependence, greed, and envy. Kernberg (1975) states that the therapist must eventually interpret split-off dependence, envy, and greed to enable the patient to integrate the split-off good and bad part objects.

There are patients who experience the separation from the bad object as a falling off into a bottomless black hole or void. This phenomenon is the ultimate manifestation of the negative therapeutic reaction. These patients have had so little good enough object relations experience in early life that the internalization of the therapist as a good object remains insufficient and fragile even after many years of treatment. When the patient begins to evidence considerable and significant separation from bad objects, there is not a strong enough internal good object to provide support. Therefore, these patients feel as if they are falling into a state of objectlessness. In terror, they cling to the bad object tenaciously, and separation is experienced as death of self or death of object.

Winnicott (1971) described the ultimate step in separation as the phantasyzed destruction of the object. The patient must phantasyze destroying the internal bad object to discover that the external object, on which it is based, has survived. For Winnicott, survival implies not only physical survival but also psychological survival—that the object neither withdraws nor retaliates. One only has to think of these B-rated horror movies in which the monster is destroyed, only to return in the sequel as even a more terrible, ferocious monster. In the paranoid-schizoid position, destruction results in the object becoming a retaliatory monster. Thus, the therapist enables the patient to distinguish the internal object from its external counterpart by surviving—neither retaliating nor withdrawing.

Through the phantasy of destroying the object, the patient becomes aware of reliving murderous impulses toward the original parental objects. It is through this late phase of treatment that the patient affectively recalls the actual traumatic and depriving experiences in early life that provoked the murderous feelings. Prior to this occurrence, the patient may describe early traumatic events, but these are sometimes intellectualized or distorted. As

71

the patient later recollects the early trauma, he also relives the early central dilemma of wanting to destroy the very objects he is absolutely dependent on for life. This is the dilemma that is relived in the transference: the wish to destroy the very object on whom he depends.

V

Working with
Severe Borderline Patients

JUSTINE

Justine is a patient I described in previous publications (1990, 1993, and 1996). She is a middle-aged married woman with an adolescent son. She initially came for treatment because she feared that she might violently abuse her child. She sometimes experienced violent and murderous impulses, which she always controlled. Her abusive tendencies related to the internalizing of the traumatic agent since she herself had been violently abused by her mother. Justine has been seen by me for eighteen years on a twice-weekly basis. She has been in therapy for much of her life since adolescence.

History and Background Information

Justine grew up in an intact, working-class family, the youngest of three children. All her siblings had histories of significant psychiatric illnesses and hospitalizations. Justine's mother was unhappy and embittered by her financial hardships and troubled marriage. The father was a withdrawn and depressed manual worker. He had grown up an orphan, and Justine had been named after his mother. Although he neglected the children, a special affinity developed between him and Justine. She escaped the violence and chaos of the family by going to him for comfort and security and felt in turn that she could help him out of his depression. All the females of the family violently abused her, which she believed resulted from their jealousy over her attachment to her father. When she was nine years old, he fondled her genitals twice.

Justine had a stormy adolescence, characterized by sexually abusive relationships with males, clinical depression, physical fighting with her mother, and suicidal gestures. She was psychiatrically hospitalized twice in adolescence for a few months on each occasion and diagnosed as a severe borderline and latent schizophrenic. She began therapy in adolescence and went through college carrying a small but manageable number of credits and then married a passive but kindly man. They had little money in that he earned a marginal salary, and she had a child shortly after finishing school.

Justine remained in treatment throughout her adolescence and terminated shortly after getting married. After having a baby, she developed postpartum depression and went to a community clinic to resume treatment. She saw a therapist for two years who helped her with her depression and abusive impulses toward her child. She was transferred to me after that therapist moved to another borough. Because she was already involved in extensive treatment, there was hardly any out of contact phase. I will describe the negative therapeutic reaction throughout the symbiotic phases as well as the prolonged resolution of symbiosis.

Question: What were the dynamics of the negative therapeutic reaction in the symbiotic phase?

Seinfeld: Before long, Justine's abusive impulses toward her child were transferred onto me, especially around separations and vacations. This resulted in Justine's discussing her history and background and describing how she had been abused and neglected. As she became involved in the transference, she felt the following manifestations. She would feel emotionally close to me, there would be a sense of attachment and libidinal excitement. As she could not act on these feelings, she would feel rejected and enraged. She then felt a sense of distance and loss, giving rise again to object hunger. She recognized that she was reliving the need for mothering and nurturance as well as the exciting and rejecting relationship with her father, which gave rise now to the wish to separate from both parents. She also described her feelings of love and hate toward the child.

Question: How did you help her contain her abusive feelings toward her child and yourself?

Seinfeld: I first took precautions to be certain she would not act on the feelings. These precautions included a psychiatric diagnostic evaluation providing her with a home care assistant and getting her assurances that she could control her impulses.

Once I was assured, I encouraged her to verbalize all her feelings and impulses. I endeavored to appear calm and blank. She said that I looked like a stone, revealing no expression or reaction. She said my response calmed her and reassured her that she was not the most terrible mother and that there was a distinction between thought and action.

Question: You described her transference reaction as exciting and rejecting. What was that like for you? What was the feeling-tone climate between you?

Seinfeld: She was one of my first difficult patients. I was not very experienced, and her previous therapist told me that she was the most difficult patient he has ever worked with. She was attractive but also hard looking. She often came in a state of emotional crisis and wanted me to explain her emotional states or how she could manage her distress. If I responded, she complained that what I said was not as helpful as the interventions of the previous therapist. She said he knew exactly what to say to calm her. If I did not respond, she said I must be intimidated and afraid that she would jump down my throat. When I said I was only getting to know her and that once I did, I might have a better idea of what to say, she said I was being defensive and it would be better if I said nothing if I did not know what to say. She wondered if she should see the director of the clinic and ask to be transferred to a new therapist. She promised that she would say not that I mistreated her but rather that I was very nice but not effective.

The above dialogue occurred over a short time with rapid-fire intensity. As a new therapist, I felt inadequate but after a while recovered enough of my capacity to think to say that she might be angry at her previous therapist for leaving and displacing that anger onto me since I remained. She laughed and said that she felt like finding him and slicing his penis into little pieces and shooting him. I said she also might be afraid of becoming involved in the treatment with me and acknowledging that I might be potentially helpful because she feared I would also leave her. She discussed her sadness and anger over the previous therapist and said she felt close to me while doing so.

Shortly thereafter, I was about to take my first vacation since seeing her. She said she felt like cutting my penis into small slices and eating it like salami. She then made her first "affectionate" comment. After she cut off my penis, she would keep it under her pillow for good luck and comfort. She also feared a shark would devour me in the ocean and then acknowledged that she was the shark.

During the exciting-rejecting object transference, she vacillated between describing fellatio phantasies and threatening to leave and never return. In the fellatio phantasies, she sometimes felt comforted and soothed like an infant sucking at a mother's breast, while at other times she felt aroused and then frustrated and angry that the fantasy could not become reality, at which point she phantasyzed biting me. There was a great suspense as to what the next session would bring. After she rejected me, I often felt incapable and wondered what I might have said or done to calm her. I was eager to see her to undo the damage. Often after rejecting me, she experienced a sense of object loss and returned wanting to merge with and devour me. Feeling inadequate and rejected, I felt reassured and excited in response to her wish for closeness. The sense of excitement and rejection was not only in her separate state of mind but became the emotional climate between us. In my own excited and rejected states of mind, I associated her attractive aspect with the exciting object and her hard aspect with the rejecting object.

Over time, the symbiotic relatedness took on a life of its own. As Justine's rejecting transference receded, the exciting transference dominated, and I felt less inadequate but more devoured. Occasionally, I responded by unconsciously distancing, sometimes with an overly intellectualized interpretation, other times by introducing the subject of her previous therapists into our discussions, thereby putting their images between her and me.

During this period, a frightening and tragic situation occurred in her life. Her young husband was stricken with a severe, immediately life-threatening and ultimately terminal illness. On the night he was suddenly taken ill, there was a huge snow blizzard. She telephoned me from the hospital, terrified as she described how he was in critical condition and hooked up on life supports while she was alone all night and without food because the hospital was short of staff because of the storm. I went to the hospital and brought her food and sat with her until we learned her husband was in less immediate danger.

After this event, Justine turned to me more readily for support and comfort, and our relationship became more therapeutically symbiotic. As her husband recovered from his acute medical crisis, Justine showed more strength with problems in hospital care, insurance, and child care than either she or I knew she had. Because of her husband's chronic illness and her precarious economic situation, Justine was under pressure to function. For the next several years, Justine struggled to become autonomous, gradually pursuing the professional world and further education and improving in her social functioning. During this period, I repeatedly interpreted her fear of becoming autonomous because she associated separation with abandonment. She was able to recall instances in childhood when her mother emotionally withdrew if she behaved autonomously but rewarded her for passive dependence. She became more independent in the transference as she reduced her weekly visits and stopped needing to telephone between sessions.

Although she was making progress, there were definite indications of anxiety. For instance, for her professional career it was necessary to take graduate courses in the evening. She completed one semester successfully but afterward repeatedly dropped courses because she felt that working and going to school were too much for her. In her tenth year of treatment, her husband's progressive medical condition took a definite turn for the worst. He quit work and went on disability, and Justine felt that all the responsibility for the family's well-being was now on her, and she felt overwhelmed. She experienced panic attacks every morning and became clinically depressed. I recommended that she see a psychopharmacologist, and she initially refused but later agreed to, as it was getting harder for her to function.

When her husband was again hospitalized and Justine learned of the worsening of his condition, she felt numb but continued to function. Only after he returned home and the situation returned to normal did she allow herself to feel the full impact of the dilemma. She could only think of what it would be like to nurse an invalid and could see no hope for the future. I interpreted that his worsening illness frightened her and therefore gave rise to anger, and she did not feel she could be angry at him because he was ill, so the anger turned against herself, causing her to feel depressed. As she verbalized her angry feelings, and especially the wish for him to die so that she would not have to take care of him as an invalid and live through the pain of waiting for him to die, she felt temporarily relieved but guilty. After a few months, she felt better, but then they had an auto accident. Her husband had been driving and was not hurt, but her back was injured.

She had to stay home for a couple of months to recover. This resulted in her feeling trapped at home with her husband, who was also depressed and angry as a result of his heart condition and being on disability. Their marital tension escalated, and after a particularly difficult quarrel, she swallowed a handful of tranquilizers "in order to end the pain." She was put into a psychiatric hospital for a brief period but then returned to the same difficult circumstances. During the next year, she made two more suicidal gestures, for which she was again hospitalized for a brief period. She felt vulnerable and depressed and that she did not have the emotional strength to withstand her difficult circumstances. She complained that her husband was constantly critical since he had become ill, and she thought of leaving him but did not feel she had the emotional strength or financial means. She also felt guilt about putting him through such stress with her depression and suicidal gestures, even though, when she was angry, she wished he was dead. Her regular antidepressant was no longer helping, so the psychopharmacologist put her on lithium—which could be fatal if taken in a suicidal gesture—on the condition that her husband hold on to the medication. She stated that often he forgot and left it available even when she was depressed and suicidal; thus, she felt he also wished her dead. I referred Justine and her husband to marital therapy, and later the husband went for individual therapy.

Question: How do you work with the projection of the internal bad object world onto the outer world when, in fact, the external circumstances are bad?

Seinfeld: Justine often felt hopeless about her life circumstances. She recounted all the hardships of her life. Her colleagues and friends often said her life was like the Book of Job. They kiddingly said she should shoot herself to put herself out of her misery. They did not realize that she was considering doing just that—ending her life—and that their remarks reinforced her feelings of hopelessness.

The difficulty in helping Justine feel more hopeful was that her life was, in reality, extremely difficult. However, it was my sense that as difficult as it was, her view of her circumstances as hopeless was colored by the projection of her own inner bad object world. One reason I believed this is that in the past I had seen Justine when her life situation was not as difficult and at times as negative and hopeless, although not for as long a time. Furthermore, when she described her current situation, she often omitted any positive factors that might provide a measure of hope.

She described her life situation not in terms of being unlucky and having more than her share of hardships but rather as an indication that she was in some way cursed and therefore persecuted. Grotstein (1994) has described how borderline patients often believe themselves to be cursed or fated. An infant who experiences itself to be protected from impingement and loved as a person in its own right thereby feels itself to be blessed. The infant, left unprotected, feels at the mercy of its own instinctive needs and environmental impingement and therefore grows to feel cursed and unwanted. Fairbairn's theory of the moral defense suggests that the infant, feeling itself to be unloved and unwanted, concludes that the mistreatment is due to its badness. In other words, the child is unworthy of being loved. The child therefore feels itself to be bad, that it is unworthy and therefore cursed. A patient such as Justine feels hopeless not only because her life circumstances are so difficult but also because her life cannot possibly improve because she is undeserving of a better life and fated to suffer. She believes bad things happen to her because she is bad. As Grotstein points out, such patients carry within a sense of original sin. Fairbairn's theory of the moral defense suggests that the original sin is not in the child's nature but rather is the internalization of the parents' badness. As Grotstein suggests, drawing on the poet William Blake, the child comes to realize that he or she is unprotected and therefore is not blessed but cursed, and this is the terrifying and terrible sense of innocence lost. The moral defense is based on an effort to deny the catastrophic disillusionment resulting from the loss of innocence.

81

When I first commented to Justine how her negative and hopeless view of reality was colored by her inner experience of negativity based on her personal history, she looked as if I were crazy and replied that anyone in her life circumstances would feel exactly as she felt. It might at first seem that her response was warranted.

> *Therapist:* Anyone in your circumstances would find it difficult, though, not everyone would feel *exactly* the same. You said once you felt cursed all your life, as if God or fate had left you at the mercy of everything that could go wrong.
>
> *Justine:* Though I don't believe in religion, I often describe my life in those terms. Whatever could possibly go wrong always does because I'm somehow being punished, cursed, or tested. When I was six, I got polio. I felt that this was a punishment or mark showing I was cursed. I don't know what for, just that I was bad in some way. I learned in therapy that I felt I was being punished for my relationship with my father. But the feeling of badness precedes even that. When my mother beat me, I felt I was bad and cursed.
>
> *Therapist:* You described your parents as overwhelmed and bitter. They often mistreated you because of their own problems. You still needed them. They were the only parents you had—so you had no recourse but to feel they treated you badly because you were bad. This left you with the belief that you were cursed and that whatever goes wrong in your life could not be that you are having more than your share of bad luck but rather that you are bad and deserved the bad things happening.

Question: The dialogue suggests a dialectical relationship between the events conditioning the patient's life and what the patient makes out of the events. Could you say more about this idea theoretically and clinically?

Seinfeld: The interpretation described previously was in response to Justine's remark that anyone would have responded exactly as she felt to her life situation. I am referring to a dialectic between traumatic conditioning and what the individual makes out of the trauma. The therapist must acknowledge the reality of the traumatic nature of the event but at the same time draw the patient's attention to her own individualized, particular response based on her own life history and internal world. Thus, the therapist responds empathetically to the fact that the patient struggles with a traumatic situation but also that her response is not inevitable and that there must be other possible feeling states and reactions to the circumstances in question. In this way, the therapist endeavors to liberate the autonomous self from the internal closed system of bad objects.

When Justine became completely hopeless about her life situation, there was nothing I or anyone could say to alleviate her depression. Adjustments of her antidepressant medication helped to a degree, but when she was in despair, both medication and therapy had little effect. At such times, Justine felt herself to be weak, helpless, and hopeless and her life situation, family, and environment as all bad. She described her husband as being constantly critical, especially when she was not depressed. She felt in pain, trapped in her life circumstances, that she no longer wished to deal with the problems in her life, and that it would be better to take her life. Sometimes her mood declined radically for no apparent reason within a few days or even hours.

I interpreted that she was trapped not only in her life circumstances but also within her internal circumstances. If she was not too depressed, she could acknowledge that her depression was brought on not only by her life circumstances but also by what was going on in her psyche. I said she was reliving in her mind all the negative experiences, and this colored how she perceived her difficult life circumstances.

Question: You have described how such patients feel possessed by internal demons. Do you refer to this phenomenon in the treatment?

Seinfeld: My priority was to determine if Justine was in fact actively suicidal, and in those periods when she was, I focused on contacting the psychiatrist and considering hospitalization. When she was not actively suicidal, I directed attention to her internal experience of demonic possession.

> *Therapist:* Your life situation is very difficult, but it is not the only thing making you depressed.
> *Patient:* This is easy for you to say.
> *Therapist:* I'm not saying it isn't difficult, but the way you are thinking about it and what is going on inside of you is another factor in your hopelessness.
> *Patient:* I can't help it. The thoughts, the depression, have a life of its own after a while. I can't just turn it off.
> *Therapist:* Describe them to me.
> *Patient:* I just keep thinking how bad it is and always was. I feel like what's the point. It never gets better.
> *Therapist:* It sounds as if you feel possessed by this depression and the negative thoughts, like they have a life of their own.
> *Patient: Possessed* is a good word. That's exactly how I feel, like I have a demon within me. I don't mean literally.

Therapist: The word *demon* is fitting. These thoughts and feelings sound demonic in the sense of how they discourage you and make you feel self-destructive and like giving up.

Patient: They make me feel like killing myself to make it stop. I feel trapped and want to run away, but there is no place to go. This is when I want to end the pain to get away.

Therapist: My sense is that the negative thoughts and feelings are a reliving of how you felt as a child in your family. You probably felt just as discouraged and persecuted by the way they treated you.

Patient: I don't recall my earliest years, but I did feel this way in latency and adolescence.

Justine recalled occasions from her childhood when she felt the same hopelessness and persecutory feelings. She wanted to run away but felt there was no place to go.

Justine: I feel that way now sometimes, especially when my husband criticizes me. I feel like leaving, but there is no place to go. I feel that way not only when others criticize me but just from the negative thoughts in my own mind. It is then that I feel like killing myself.

Therapist: When you felt persecuted and mistreated as a child, you probably felt murderous feelings toward your parents and wanted to run away—not only from them but from your own anger toward them. Now their influence is inside you. You feel the same sense of persecution from your own thoughts or feelings representing your parents. Therefore, when you feel the impulse to kill yourself, I think you are reliving the early wish to kill your parents. However, now these parents are felt to be within you, so you feel the wish to kill them within you. Remember before you described how you felt possessed by a demon.

Justine: Please don't use the word *demon*. I know I used it before, but it makes me nervous, as if I might really be possessed. I know you don't mean it literally, but I begin to feel that way.

The next day Justine reported the following dream that made her extremely anxious. She dreamt that she was in hell, surrounded by male and female demons. There were snakes and flames surrounding her, and then she woke up. She said that the dream was vivid and real. On her job the next day, she continually recalled the dream and at times felt she actually might be in hell. I again reiterated that we were talking not about real demons but about the internal influence of her parents as well as how she imagined them to be and her rage at them. It is their internal influence and her own rage that feels demonic. I attempted to help her intellectualize this so that she would not be overcome with psychotic anxieties about distinguishing fantasy and reality. I described how the great Dante had vivid and poetic dreams of demons and transformed them into his great epic about hell, and I informed her of the term *bad objects* as the scientific designation for the internal influence of her parents. She disliked the term *bad objects* even more than demons, saying it is too clinical and sounds even more as if it referred to "nut cases." She preferred the term *demons,* so long as she kept in mind that it represented the internal parents and not real demons.

It was my sense that the internal demons were becoming more vivid, real, and intense because they were emerging from repression. Fairbairn (1943) compared therapy to exorcism in that the goal is to release bad objects from the unconscious.

Question: Why does the psychic system become closed to change?

Seinfeld: Sutherland (1994) has remarked that the distinguished American existential philosopher William Barrett has come to important conclusions about psychic functioning that closely resemble the views of object relations theory, even though he is unfamiliar with that theory. In discussing existential theory, Barrett (1979) states, "For what is the depressing sense of unfreedom that steals over us at times but the feeling that the world has closed in on us, that we are in a prison all the doors of which have been locked, and that we are trapped in a routine that never opens up any fresh possibilities."

This philosophical depiction of a world closing in on and entropying the individual accords exactly with Justine's depiction of her depression. Sutherland asserts the important theoretical formulation that the thwarting of the autonomous self and freedom is the ultimate source of the arousal of hatred. Thus, Justine is reliving her parents' early thwarting of the autonomous self and the arousal of hatred now turned against the self.

Fairbairn (1958) rejected Freud's theory of the death instinct but acknowledged the common presence of self-destructiveness. Fairbairn, however, attributed this self-destructiveness to the inclination, on the part of the patient, to maintain aggression localized within the confines of the inner world as a closed psychic system. Furthermore, this aggression is directed also against libidinal need, thereby driving the patient to seek such satisfaction as can be achieved within the closed system of the inner world. Thus, to Fairbairn, disappointment in experiencing satisfaction with external objects results in rage—and this rage is directed inward, against the subject's own libidinal need that has been disappointed—and also in an effort to keep the inner world closed at all costs. The individual is thereby protected from further disappointment by the outer world but at the same time feels hopeless over the possibility of achieving satisfaction or change in relationships with external objects.

The original failure to achieve satisfactory object relations may be so traumatic as to create and perpetuate the obstruction of the autonomous self in the experience of being trapped within a closed psychic system that negates freedom to interact with the world. The autonomous self will have no way to express itself except through actively perpetuating the closed internal system and relating to the outer world according to the negative expectations of the inner world. The aim of treatment is to effect a breach in the closed psychic system so that the patient can be open to change from the influence of outer reality.

Justine had made considerable progress in functioning, as she gradually was able to work full time to support herself and her family and to take part-time courses. At this point, she became profoundly depressed and had great difficulty functioning. The worsening of her husband's medical condition also contributed to her depression. She received this bad news about his condition just as she was beginning to feel more autonomous and successful. She always associated the achievement of autonomy with the threat of inevitable object loss. This threat brought to her mind a flood of memories of how she felt, as a child, that her mother threatened her with abandonment and withdrawal whenever she tried to function autonomously.

Thus, as she functioned more autonomously and feared losing her husband, she relived the early abandonment anxiety associated with her mother threatening to abandon her. But something even more terrifying could be felt beneath her abandonment anxiety—that if she became autonomous and separated from the bad object that held her back, there would be no good object to replace them with; thus, she would fall into the void of object-lessness. She said, "There is something about functioning autonomously that strikes a core of terror in me that is beyond anything

I can put into words. It is a feeling of such aloneness and despair. It is being deserted, but it is even more than that. It is like falling into a black hole of despair, that is the only way I can describe it."

Thus, as she made enough progress to be on the verge of becoming truly more autonomous, she suffered extreme anxiety from separating from her bad objects and therefore desperately returned to them. Her anxiety was also based on the fact that her aged mother, who resided in a nursing home, was becoming increasingly frail and infirm. Justine not only experienced herself as afraid to separate from bad objects but also experienced her bad objects as terrified that she would separate. For instance, she dreamt that her mother was ill and Justine was planning to take a trip. The mother said, "How could you go when you know I'm dying?" The mother then began to bleed profusely. In a second dream that same evening, Justine was herself ill and hemorrhaging uncontrollably and was terrified that she was dying. In a third dream, she owed her employer money and had to pay it back and therefore could not take the trip. This dream of difficult financial considerations holding her back was reflected in her real life in that she had run up so much credit on shopping that she was in considerable debt and had to declare personal bankruptcy. Thus, the dreams illustrated that she was identified with the internal mother and that if she tried to separate, one or both would die. The third dream reflected how, in her actual life, she was acting self-defeating to thwart separation.

When she acted self-defeating—for instance, by dropping out of a course or by running up her credit—she would attack herself for her "stupidity." I would respond, "The problem is not that you are stupid. By attacking yourself as stupid, you are not trying to become more autonomous but instead perpetuating the feeling that you are too stupid to become autonomous. It is one thing to look at this behavior and to try to understand it. But that is not what you are doing. When you call yourself names, you just become more depressed. It is as if you did something to give yourself another reason to beat up on yourself."

Gradually, Justine was able to see that her attacks against herself were an expression of her "inner demons" and another way to hold on to her bad objects. As she tenaciously held on to her bad objects, she felt more persecuted by them. She increasingly became aware that when she felt depressed and self-destructive, she was really feeling enraged and destructive toward her persecutors.

Question: Even after clients understand the origins and nature of their internal bad objects, they often continue to feel tortured and persecuted. Is there anything the client or therapist can do to actively exorcise bad objects?

Seinfeld: The clinician should encourage the client to actively psychically spit out the bad objects. As mentioned earlier, aggression has been confined to the closed psychic system along with bad objects. Understanding and analyzing the nature and function of bad objects does not necessarily release this aggression. Thus, it may be necessary for the therapist to actively encourage the patient to aggressively kick out the bad objects. At one point, I said to Justine, "The only way you know how to say 'fuck you' to your persecutors is by hurting yourself. Another way of saying 'fuck you' and of freeing yourself is by trying to make a life where you are free of them and trying to enjoy and improve the quality of your life." She replied, "I've heard it said that success is the best revenge. I guess you mean something like that."

There were times when Justine could feel such profound despair and be so dominated by her bad objects that she could not perceive any hope whatsoever that there could be anything good to her life. I would respond, "It is true that the world could be pretty bad and that for you it is often very bad. However, your belief is that the world is all bad, that there is no possibility of anything good happening and therefore that there is nothing to hope for except inner demons. They are telling you not to separate, not to have any faith in any goodness in the world so that you will remain tied to them. The world is pretty bad sometimes, but it is not all bad. You are now reliving the terror of separating from your parents and the projection of all the negative aspects of that relationship into the world."

There were occasions when she felt like killing the negative feelings and thoughts emanating and persecuting her from within, and there were other times when she experienced the persecutory thoughts as convincing her that there was no hope and she should end her life. I interpreted that the internal demons were now telling her to kill herself, that they were obstructing her efforts to separate and wanted to discourage her at all costs. On a couple of occasions when she was feeling especially persecuted and hopeless, I told her to tell the internal demons to stop torturing her, to leave her be, that she does not deserve such abuse. Justine replied, "But the demons are not real. You are telling me to address them as if they are real."

> *Therapist:* That is correct. They are definitely not real. But you experience all you feel as real. That's the point. What I refer to as demons are experiences you have internalized that you mistakenly experience as real.
>
> *Justine:* I lose sight of that. It feels ingrained like the only way I could possibly be who I am.
>
> *Therapist:* That's it. It's not ingrained, it's internalized. What we are calling demons and bad objects are attitudes you have internalized that color your view of yourself and the world. You could potentially or theoretically get rid of them right now in this session. I know that is not so

91

easy, and you can't cast them out immediately as if they are demons. The point is they are not who you are but what you have taken in.

Justine: I see what you are saying. I never thought of it like that. It is these attitudes that stop me from being autonomous and make me feel I can't be—that I'm either too bad or the world is too bad. When you told me to tell the demons to leave me alone, I thought we were doing an exorcism—a Jewish exorcism. Just kidding.

In encouraging the patient to exorcise or be rid of bad objects, the aim is not for the patient to be entirely rid of bad objects but rather to be able to fight off the persecution until the patient is finally able to integrate good and bad objects. This integration cannot fully occur until the good object has become strong enough to be dominant. Until this time, the patient must at least know how to fight off persecutory objects aggressively so that she does not succumb to the persecution.

Question: How does the patient's despair and hopelessness affect the therapist? Countertransference? How is the counter-transference managed?

Seinfeld: The greatest difficulty for the therapist in working with the patient who is seeing the world through the hopelessness of bad objects is that the therapist, seeing the world through empathy with the patient's despair, will come to feel as hopeless as the patient. The patient only describes the negative aspects of her situation and is not even aware of whatever positive aspects there may be. Thus, the therapist only hears how bad and hopeless the patient's situation is, and the therapist might feel as if he or she is falling into a black hole with the patient.

Eigen (1993) states that the borderline patient experiencing paranoid-schizoid splitting often undergoes an impending sense of catastrophe associated with ego growth. Thus, as the patients separate and feel more vulnerable in relation to the persecutory objects, as their rage is aroused in reliving early trauma, they express to the therapist the sense that the catastrophe is imminent and that every hardship threatens to become a catastrophe. Thus, the therapist must contain the patient's sense of despair and catastrophe.

When Justine presented how hopeless she was, how her depression would never be alleviated, I had to struggle not only with her despair and how bad she felt her life was but also with my own sense of how hopeless her life was.

In one session, Justine told me how her depression and despair would never be alleviated. She sat silent and remorsefully waited for my response. I sat silently as well, and she said that this was one of the few occasions when I was at a loss for words. I replied that she was feeling hopeless and trying to get me to share in that feeling.

> *Therapist:* I think when you feel so hopeless, you feel all alone. You imagine me going on my way with whatever I am doing, so you are trying to convey to me your hopelessness so we both feel that way.
>
> *Justine:* But I also feel like you're giving up, like you're fed up and giving up.
>
> *Therapist:* When you came in and said how hopeless you felt and that nothing could help, I felt that you were giving up. I think you were giving up. I think you are trying to make me feel that way—like giving up. You are presenting a case for how hopeless it is—you are fed up.
>
> *Justine:* I see what you are saying. I do feel like giving up. I'm attributing to you what I'm feeling. I'm trying to make you feel that way. I wonder why.

93

Therapist: I don't know. It seems you are angry with me. You are in this hopeless situation, and I'm not doing anything to rescue you, so you are fed up and feel like giving up.

Justine: I don't expect you to rescue me. I know that is not possible.

Therapist: You do not expect me to rescue you in terms of what you know intellectually. You've been in therapy long enough to know that is not my role. But emotionally you may wish it. After all, your difficult situation would evoke childlike feelings of hopelessness and helplessness in anyone. In fact, anyone in your situation would wish to be rescued. You don't have much money. Your husband is terminally ill. You're depressed. Since I'm the person you've come to for help, it makes sense you would wish for me to rescue you. You convey this wish when you feel so hopeless, helpless, and that a catastrophe might occur. It may be that you are unconsciously trying to communicate how much you need to be rescued. Then maybe some of your depression is your anger at me turned against yourself because I don't rescue you.

Justine: I certainly could use rescuing. I sometimes fantasize some rich man will come along to rescue me. I don't think of you that way. I mean as rescuing me, I see what you are saying. Unconsciously, I might wish that you'd rescue me and might be expressing this through my suicidal gestures.

When Justine became despairing, hopeless, and suicidal, she did not desperately reach out but instead withdrew and became disconnected. During these occasions, she could not feel any connection with me or with anyone. I stated that during her life the negative experience so outweighed the positive experience that when she became overwhelmed, there was little in the way of comforting memories or feelings to draw on. Therefore, she could not bring herself to believe that anyone in her life, including me, could help.

Fairbairn (1958) stated that the severely disturbed patients dominated by internal bad objects could become closed off to the outer world. I would add that this is not only because of bad objects but also because of the lack of a good enough internal object that would provide the patient with enough hope to believe that the world is not all bad and that some good, comforting, or sustaining experience could come from it. Fairbairn stated that the aim of psychotherapy is to effect a breach in the closed inner world of the patient. In this way, the internal world can be influenced and modified by reality. The therapist must begin to be internalized as a good object for the patient to feel enough trust or faith that there could be some support in the outer world. Fairbairn believed that the actual relationship between the patient and therapist is the decisive factor in effecting therapeutic results. As Sutherland (1989) notes, Fairbairn was an unusually conservative man in all areas of life, with the exception of psychoanalytic theory building. Therefore, he was quite cautious in advancing any innovations in therapeutic technique based on theory. However, Fairbairn (1958) acknowledged his essentially conservative disposition and suggested that his theoretical formulations did have implications for the future in the development of technique.

Fairbairn stated, "It may seem strange that hitherto I have made only the scantiest reference in print to the implications of my theoretical formulations for the practice of psychoanalytic treatment. From this fact it may be inferred that, even in my opinion, my views are of merely theoretical interest and their implementation in practice would leave the technique of psychoanalysis unaffected. Such an inference would be quite unwarranted. The fact being that the practical implications of my views

95

have seemed so far-reaching that they could only be put to the test gradually, and with the greatest circumspection if premature or rash psychotherapeutic conclusions were to be concluded."

It is my opinion that Fairbairn was correct in adopting this conservative approach for the development of technique. He believed that technique based on his theory should develop gradually, not radically; thus, I would suggest that the theoretical view that the closed psychic system is based not only on the dominance of inner bad objects but also on the lack of inner good objects warrants that the therapist may be more active and reach out to effect a breach in the closed system.

Justine understood my remarks that she lacked enough supportive experience to internalize a belief that the world was not all bad but rather both good and bad. Nevertheless, she could not overcome her tendency to withdraw during these periods. It was therefore necessary for me to be more active in reaching out to effect a breach in the closed system. When Justine was extremely despondent, I arranged for us to have telephone contact between sessions explaining that I was aware that in such states, she lost her connection to myself and the outer world and therefore felt isolated and hopeless. The central issue was that she was separating from bad objects and did not have a sufficiently internalized good object. She therefore felt as if she were falling into an existential black hole and needed more contact. However, Justine's withdrawal had to do not only with the lack of an internal good object but also with transferential conflicts that grew greater as she experienced more emotional contact.

The fundamental therapeutic approach to Fairbairn's premise is that the therapist must be a good enough object in reality for the patient to release her bad objects. I would elaborate on this premise by suggesting that the therapist must actively provide good object experience for the patient to feel safe enough to fully activate the bad object transference. The implication of Fairbairn's theory is that the major therapeutic effect is in the release of the bad object transference while the therapist remains in reality a good enough object. In this way, the patient can separate from the internal bad object.

Question: How is the bad object transference manifested and worked through?

Seinfeld: As Justine started to feel reconnected in the transference, she became aware that her wish to be rescued was directed toward me. For instance, she fantasized that we would run off together and that I would take her away from her miserable life circumstances. These fantasies did have an oedipal erotic component, but she experienced this as secondary to the wish for comfort, holding, and protection. She then acknowledged that these fantasies were always in the back of her mind—she had them more intensely in the first part of her treatment, but she pushed them to the back of her mind as she forced herself to function and work. She felt that they were now coming to the fore because she was growing more anxious as she became more autonomous. She said that the fantasy was disturbing not only because of the erotic element but even more because she started to feel enraged and there was no possibility of acting on it.

Fairbairn described the bad internal object situation as constituted by an exciting, nongratifying and a rejecting punitive object. Thus, Justine's transference emerged as a full-blown bad object transference; the exciting object that she wished would rescue her from her miserable life circumstances and the rejecting object that would not act out with her. She said she experienced ambivalence about my not rescuing her—the fact that I cared enough about her treatment to protect it made her feel full of gratitude, but she also felt enraged that I did not act out with her erotically. She acknowledged having a hard time holding on to her ambivalent feelings. She realized it was something she never could do and that she therefore always saw others as either all good or all bad. She now decided to make an active effort to feel connected to me while feeling angry. She realized that when she withdrew, she felt disconnected, and the anger at me turned against herself. This is what Fairbairn (1958) meant when he described how in the closed internal system, the aggression at objects in the outer world turned inward, repressing libidinal need, thereby giving rise to isolation, hopelessness, and self-destructiveness. By simultaneously experiencing her libidinal need and anger toward the transference object, there is opportunity for the libidinal and antilibidinal selves to become integrated with the central self.

As Justine experienced the erotic transference, she became aware that her fantasies corresponded to her experience with her father. She wished to sit on my lap and to be held exactly as she had been held by her father. She fantasized that I would fondle her genitals as her father had. She became enraged at her father for violating her, but she became enraged at me for not doing so and frustrating her. She said her anger at her father was not only because of his inappropriate behavior but also because he did not care enough about her as a child to restrain himself from behavior he knew to be harmful. However, it was very troubling for her to be angry with him. It was easier for her to be angry with her mother for violently abusing her. She said her mother, for the most part, always mistreated her. The situation with her father was more complicated. The little love or support she received was from him. For most of her life, that was her sole source of self-esteem. To give this up might mean she would be left with nothing. She was most troubled because she recognized that even the good part of him that comforted and supported her felt good but was not so good, that he did it for his own needs, and this led to his behaving destructively.

She often found herself making excuses for him. She would remind herself that he had a difficult marriage, a troubled childhood, that his relationship to Justine was the only comfort in his life. At such times, she noted that she felt comforted feeling close to him but more depressed as she started to feel it was her fault he behaved as he did. She felt less depressed when she realized her parents were poor parents, but then she began to feel all alone and made excuses for her father.

During this period, her mother, who had been ill and infirm, died. At first, she felt released. She imagined her mother burning in hell and felt a sense of satisfaction. However, after a time, she began to feel sorry for her mother's hard life, that she herself had given her mother a hard time, that her mother had a difficult period before her death. Justine felt again that she was at fault, that she did not deserve to live a rewarding life in that her mother had suffered and died. She began to feel responsible for her parents' abuse and mistreatment of her. She would become despairing and suicidal. I responded that only her parents were responsible for their abuse of her, that they were poor parents, and that though they did have a hard life, that did not excuse their mistreatment of her and she did have a right to be angry. I explained I was saying not that they were bad as people but that they were inadequate parents and she suffered because of it. Because she needed them, she excused them for their abusive behavior and blamed herself, saying they treated her as worthless because she was unworthy. She continued to blame herself for everything that went wrong in her life, seeing this as evidence that she is bad at the core and deserves persecution.

Destroying and Rediscovering the Object

Justine realized that if she attempted to fill the void by internalizing me, she had to deal with her ambivalence—feeling connected but angry. When she held on to her idealized father, she

99

avoided ambivalence. He was all good, but she was bad and therefore depressed. As she attempted to separate, she felt threatened by objectlessness, as if she was falling into a black hole. I asked what happened to her relationship with me when she fell into the void. She replied that if she brought me there, she would want to kill me. I suggested she take my image with her so as not to be all alone. At this point, she began to experience the phantasy of destroying me but discovering I was still there in reality for her use. Winnicott described how the client needs to experience the destruction and survival of the therapist to discover externality.

VI

Intersubjective Aspects in the Treatment of Schizoid Patients

EDWARD

Edward called in late spring one year ago requesting treatment. I was reluctant to respond because I was leaving for vacation in August. I returned his call somewhat later than it would typically take me. He sounded eager to be seen, so I agreed to meet for a consultation, stating that I might not have the time to continue but would refer him elsewhere.

Edward was Arabic and Islamic and came to the United States in his early twenties. He was in his mid-thirties, studying science. While in the Middle East, he met with one of the few psychologists who had some psychoanalytic training in the West. He described himself as functioning adequately in his professional life but that underneath he experienced great despair. He read a book on clinical psychology and recognized that he suffered from many of the described symptoms, so he sought help. After a couple of years of treatment, his therapist told him his problems were very deep and related to the earliest stages of development and that he therefore needed a Kleinian or object relations type of treatment. When he arrived in the United States, he continued to feel depressed and sought out a psychologist. The latter convinced him to undergo psychological testing and afterward stated that the Rorschach test indicated that he was profoundly disturbed and suffered from a schizoid core. I said that since the test was developed in the West, it might not accurately assess someone from his culture. He laughed and said that he would be crazy in the context of his own culture as well.

He said he was shopping around for a therapist and had taken several names off the Internet. He was scheduled for two more consultations and would call after completing them.

Question: How did this patient make a choice of therapists? What was the relationship between his choice and the issues of resistance and psychic structure?

Seinfeld: Edward called me and asked for another appointment. He said he would select me for a therapist if I would work with him. It is often thought by clinicians that patients choose therapists for their good listening skills, empathy, perceptiveness, and so forth. Unfortunately, these are not the reasons Edward chose me. He said he believed I was not very interested in working with him. I asked how he came to this conclusion, and he said it took me longer than it took the other clinicians to return his calls. He also found my attitude and behavior during the session to be less formal, less structured, and less serious. I asked him to elaborate, and he said I laughed when he said he has a schizoid core and would be crazy in his own culture. The therapists were serious, asked him about his symptoms, and took careful notes. I asked why he was choosing me. He said one of the therapists was so eager to see him that he was concerned the therapist was money hungry. The other therapist exuded warmth and empathy and made him feel as if he was pitiable.

Over the first few weeks of treatment, he told me about his history and current life situation. I asked him how he experienced our relationship now that he was getting to know me, and he said he can talk freely but still feels I might not like him and might not be interested. He did appreciate that I encouraged him to tell me this. I asked what made him feel that I was not too interested, and he said I sometimes seemed to forget some of the facts he told me. I asked what his experience had been with his previous therapist in the Middle East. He said it was entirely different. He had the idea, which the therapist later confirmed, that he was one of a very few patients the psychologist saw. Therefore, the therapist was very interested and even encouraged him to become a psychologist himself. Edward had the idea that the psychologist was looking for a follower and disciple. When Edward chose to study natural science instead, he felt the psychologist was disappointed and started to lose interest in him. I asked if he discussed this with the therapist, and he said no.

In terms of resistance and psychic structure, it is likely that Edward selected me because his antidependent self was less threatened by my seemingly not too interested stance. It is possible that if I had appeared too interested and engaging, it would have brought too much to mind his former therapist, who had been so interested and then withdrew. Therefore, it was less likely that he would become so involved, only to be disappointed later. This analysis of the resistance does not imply that the therapist should deliberately set out to be disinterested. There was no way I could have known that he had been disappointed by the abrupt loss of interest of his previous therapist. In fact, I found him interesting enough to take on as a patient at a time of year that I did not want to do anymore work but was preparing for vacation.

Question: How do intersubjective factors become manifest in resistance and counterresistance?

Seinfeld: When patients express how my stance is affecting their relationship, I always encourage them to pursue an analysis of my behavior and motivations. I do so whether patients feel I seem uninterested, too interested, or whatever else. I asked Edward to freely speak of all the reasons I might dislike him or be uninterested in him. He came up with several possibilities and then said that he imagines that with a name like Seinfeld, I must be Jewish. I acknowledged this was so. He wondered if I might not like him for this reason. I asked what went into his decision to choose me thinking I was Jewish. He said it did not matter to him, that he is a nonpracticing, nonreligious Muslim. I asked him if he could describe more of his concerns about how I, as a Jew, might dislike him for being Islamic. He said I might think he hates me. I might be frightened of him. I might think he is a terrorist. I laughed and said maybe he is an Arab terrorist out to get New York City Jewish therapists.

He appeared significantly more relaxed and said, "I actually doubt that you don't like me because I'm Arab-Islamic. You are an educated man who has written respected books in your profession. It appears you would be liberal and logical and not prejudiced."

I commented that although we share liberal outlooks concerning our heritages, we were nevertheless brought up in cultures that consider one another adversaries and enemies and it is important to remember that these attitudes are internalized and could subtly affect how we relate to each other or color our feelings about each other. We agreed to keep this area open for future discussion.

Edward wondered whether his initial belief that I was disinterested or did not like him was correct. Maybe he did not like me because I took my time calling him back. He wondered why I took so long. I said, "My reactions have nothing to do with whether I like you or not. Summer was beginning, and I was not eager to engage in more work. Now this doesn't mean I like you—or dislike you. I might like you, or I might dislike you, but either way I didn't feel like beginning any more work."

Question: Treatment with schizoid patients is typically characterized by a sense of boredom, deadness, and futility in the transference-countertransference. How does the therapist address this?

Seinfeld: Edward has a great deal of difficulty initiating each session. I encouraged him to discuss this, and he replied he is not a "man of words." He described himself as feeling as if he is enveloped with a plastic covering with an opening only for his mouth. Within this plastic envelopment, he and the world feel unreal, as if he is semi-asleep, waiting to be awakened. He experiences us as very far apart—his plastic covering places him on another planet. He said he can observe the two of us with great detachment. I asked what he observes. He said my mind reminds him of a vessel with thoughts and feelings bubbling around. When I come to the session, I have to quiet my mind, which is so active it threatens to bubble over. He feels it takes me a while to quiet it, but then I am in a receptive state. He said his mind is the opposite. It is constricted, everything is closed in, it is tight—like a mental constipation.

I said, "So here we are. You psychically constipated and me psychically boiling over." He said it is as if he has a gem or treasure inside that he does not want to lose. I asked what this could be about. He said he feels great psychic hunger, maybe hunger for love. He asked if I saw *Silence of the Lambs*. He said the protagonist devoured and chewed people up. Edward felt he did something like that psychically. It is as if he has a fantasy of having something precious within that he has devoured. He recalled a number of love relationships in which he felt he did not really need the other because he felt he had this loving person inside of him. It feels like the love of a woman, so he imagines it is a maternal thing. When he told his former therapist of this, the latter said he could use Kleinian analysis.

After describing this sense of something precious inside, Edward continued to have difficulty speaking. He described his life not as a continuing narrative but rather in disjointed fragments. He said it was difficult to talk about himself. He never reacted to anything immediately. It was as if anything that occurred had to be processed through a bureaucracy of his mind before it finally registered. He never knew how he felt immediately or what to make of any incident that occurred. He said he imagines that this is what is meant by dissociation. He felt a sense of envy that I was immediate in my responses. It was not that my response was extreme in any way; rather, he felt that I was affected and alive. If he participated and was entertaining, I was clearly engaged. When he had difficulty speaking and felt out of touch, he could sense I was bored. If he was talking circuitously and not getting into things, he felt my frustration. He felt I had an immediate response, whereas he never did.

I asked if he could say what affect best characterized this therapy. He said boredom. He was not sure which of us was most responsible. When he labored to speak, it appeared that I labored to listen. I asked if he could describe in detail what he saw in me that he read this way. He said often I yawn and become fidgety. He said when he is bored, he is detached to the point where the other ceases to exist. I asked if I could be contributing to the boring atmosphere. He said he sometimes feels angry and believes I should try hard to make my reactions less obvious. He was not sure if my response was really so obvious or whether the degree of his dissociation made any kind of reaction seem extreme. However, I did yawn and often forgot what he told me. He said he was confused about me. I made it really comfortable for him to talk and never seemed to judge anything, but there was this disinterest.

I asked if he had any thoughts about why I might be disinterested. He recalled how he had told me how he had tortured his cat after it favored his visiting friend over him. This incident was the one time he felt I was judgmental because I expressed more concern about his cat than I had ever expressed about him. He wondered if there wasn't some detachment over the Jewish-Muslim factor. Maybe I was not interested in him because of his heritage.

As a child, he often fantasized about destroying Israel. He ceased having this fantasy and grew up, but in the past two months the fantasy has returned. He imagines he receives a divine message and inspiration to create a high-tech aerial force to attack Israel. He has the attack launched, and it results in Israel's surrender. Israel is now forced to listen to the Islamic point of view.

He stated that even though he came from a family of dissidents that denounced the government, they nevertheless disliked Israel because they believed the constant tension between Israel and the other Middle Eastern countries allowed those governments to justify oppressive measures and demands in the name of the war with Israel. Now that these childhood fantasies were returning, he wondered whether he did not seek out a Jewish therapist so he could deal with some of these feelings from childhood. I replied that it could work in both directions simultaneously—that he could have sought out a Jewish therapist to deal with some of these issues and that some of these issues may be coming up because of his feelings about his Jewish therapist. He said he must be equating me with Israel. I said that the oppressive government of his childhood represents the internal persecutory parents and I represent Israel that he feels not only did not help but made things worse. I said he also may feel quite disloyal telling his problems to Israel—this may be a factor in his difficulty talking.

He told me he was not going to be coming in for a session next week, and I forgot. Therefore, when he did not arrive, I called his answering machine, saying I was waiting for him and wondered why he did not arrive. He called directly before his next appointment to tell me he was coming in and also that he had said he had to be away the previous week. When he came in, he laughed and said, "You forgot that I had told you I wasn't coming."

I said yes and asked how he felt about it. He said he thought it was funny and felt relieved. It made him feel that maybe I do not forget because I am disinterested in him, maybe I forget simply because there is something wrong with me. We agreed that we would monitor my forgetting in the next weeks and see if it gets worse or better.

He said he was telling a friend during the week about his therapy with me. He described to his friend how he analyzes his therapy, and his friend believed this was peculiar. He told his friend it was actually very helpful. Whenever he is speaking to the person in a polite, respectful, superficial way, on the other hand, he is thinking all sorts of critical things about the person that he would never dare to say. He said this goes on in every single relationship he has, and it is only in this experience in therapy that he has told the other person everything he is thinking. Since doing so, this relationship is beginning to feel real and alive. The friend asked Edward how the therapist responds, and Edward said he laughs and plays around with what I say. Then Edward proceeded to tell his friend some critical thoughts he had about him that he never before had said, and the friend responded favorably. Edward concluded that he believed that relating felt so dead and boring because he never before expressed his true thoughts about the other.

In our next session, Edward began by saying our chairs seemed closer together. I took my chair and moved with it to a point farther away from Edward and said we could sit this far apart but I doubt it would solve the problem. I brought my chair back to its original spot and said the chairs are the same distance apart as always—the problem is you are feeling closer to me today. He replied that is correct; in the last few sessions, he is even feeling that I like him and he feels I am interested. He said this is embarrassing because it brings to mind an image of childhood. He recalls the bathroom door being open and he fleetingly sees his father urinating, and he has a remembrance of his father's penis seeming large and powerful. He is now having an abstract thought of eating my penis. He said this is all vague and abstract, but there is this sense of connection to me somehow taking this form. He recalled telling me how he felt hungry for love. Now there was this vague notion of taking something of me in. In subsequent sessions, he was able to engage and interact with greater ease.

This patient's negative therapeutic reaction is manifested in a sense of deadness and boredom. Ferenczi has described how the traditional therapeutic posture of formal, detached politeness can contribute to the patient feeling uneasy about expressing critical thoughts to the therapist. Ferenczi believed many patients experienced critical thoughts about the therapist but did not express them for fear of injuring and angering the therapist.

Thus, the patient responds to the therapist's polite, formal manner in kind. Edward experienced this splitting off of negative thoughts from his external relations throughout his life. Thus, all his relationships seemed flat and dead. The boring deadness soon permeates our therapeutic situation. By discussing the cultural differences between us, a framework was prepared for Edward to express his critical thoughts. When he first came to treatment, I always thought of him as my Middle Eastern Islamic patient, indicating that I did see him through the lens of whatever an Islamic Middle Easterner meant to a New York Jew despite my best liberal intentions. I was not aware of any conscious prejudicial or hostile thoughts, but at first I did wonder if he would think I was prejudiced against him and wondered if he was prejudiced against me, implying that what I had internalized concerning an Islamic Middle Easterner was part of my own cultural countertransference. Discussing this issue between us resulted in both of us feeling greater freedom to discuss any of the issues that arose in our relationship.

I did not go out of my way to suppress my own bored reaction to his laborious presentation. I do not mean to say that I was deliberately or grossly provocative in my responses. He was able to read my countertransference. I encouraged him to do so, and then we were able to discuss the boredom between us. I never responded by asking the patient, "What are you doing to make me bored?" Rather, this affect is something between the patient and myself and must be discussed as what is going on between us. I believe whatever affect pervades the negative therapeutic reaction should somehow be brought up for discussion, whether it is hopelessness, apathy, boredom, excitement, depression, or whatever. In working with detached schizoid patients, I am likely to manifest a negative countertherapeutic reaction in the form of forgetting. I keep a very busy schedule and must make a special effort not to forget daily happenings. But this is something I am also quite capable of doing outside any negative reaction to a patient. Once this patient expressed his critical thoughts about me, he presented a fellatio fantasy. I have found in working with male and female patients alike that the patients frequently experience internalizing the therapist through a sexual fantasy after verbalizing anger. If the therapist is accepting of the anger, he or she becomes a potentially good enough object that the patient wishes to take in.

The schizoid patient suffers from anxiety over loss of self. Existentialism describes this phenomenon as ontological insecurity. The individual feels unreal, an inner deadness, and a lack of vitality and spontaneity. There is no sense of genuine being and aliveness. Compulsive doing and frantic activity can cover an insecure foundation of being. These patients have often suffered from an inordinate degree of familial impingement and intrusiveness. The following clinical vignette will illustrate how the therapist endeavors to engage the client in an authentic therapeutic experience. Those patients often manifest the negative therapeutic reaction by creating an apathetic, superficial, and disengaged affective climate. They do not manifest the love and hate of the borderline client or the impulsive flight enactment of the out of contact client but instead evoke a false self-transference–countertransference situation. The negative therapeutic reaction of these patients is not easily recognizable because the treatment is not affectively intense or difficult. Instead, there is a feeling that nothing is happening, the sessions seem boring, and the patient and therapist feel disengaged from each other. The therapeutic relationship does not feel real or alive. Severely schizoid patients often detach themselves from the therapeutic process to protect themselves from impingement.

Question: What occurs in the therapeutic process that threatens the schizoid self with impingement?

111

Seinfeld: Winnicott stressed that there is a part of the self that inevitably and inherently needs to remain secret and private. The secret self experiences becoming known as a violation and impingement. The implication of the universal secret self is that there is an adaptive, positive side of the patient's resistance. Furthermore, no matter how empathic, sensitive, or knowledgeable the therapist is, the treatment process is always something of a threat to the patient's need for privacy. The therapist must remain empathic to the patient's experience as therapy being intrusive.

The problem is compounded in the treatment of the severely schizoid patient. The natural and inevitable therapeutic process of the patient's self-disclosure is a threat to the only way the schizoid has been able to protect a fragile sense of self-by-self concealment. It is this threat that provokes the negative therapeutic reaction. In the treatment of seriously schizoid patients, the negative therapeutic reaction is manifested in a climate that has become unreal, disengaged, and apathetic. Client and/or therapist may forget what was discussed in previous sessions, forget scheduled appointments, and so forth, as I described in the previous case example.

The following clinical vignette will illustrate the first session of treatment with a seriously schizoid client.

Question: How does the therapist address the defenses of depersonalization and derealization?

Seinfeld: Ellen telephoned to request therapy, stating she had read one of my books and felt that my description of schizoid states fit her perfectly. She had friends who were therapists, and they told her about my writings.

She appeared relaxed and walked gracefully into my office, so I was surprised that the first few minutes of discussion were tense and labored. She described her psychic distress in a detached, theoretical manner to the extent that I felt I was listening to a recording of my own book. I commented on the theoretical presentation of her clinical case, and she laughed and said she had been in therapy but it never worked out because she did not speak from the heart. I commented that her presentation had an unreal quality—not that I believed she was being deceitful but rather that she sounded quite detached from the psychic states she described. She said the term *unreal* was quite fitting to describe how she felt.

She said this entire experience felt unreal. She experienced herself, me, and the office setting as unreal. She said my office could be a movie set for a scene depicting therapy. I laughed and pointed at the matching chairs, leather couch, and desk strewn with papers and my telephone and acknowledged that we could be actors playing the parts of therapist and patient. She pointed to my antique Chinese lamp and Indian paintings and said that she liked both. I told her that those were the pieces I enjoyed as well, but I was unable to make the rest of the office as aesthetically pleasing while maintaining the appearance of a therapy setting. She said she actually liked my office—it was comfortable. She said her own apartment was aesthetically pleasing, but it was not comfortable because she hardly had any furniture. She proceeded to describe her personal history and how she felt traumatic familial events resulted in her current troubles. Her descriptions of herself and her life were more fragmented and chaotic, but she clearly seemed more authentic and comfortable toward the end of our session. I asked her how she experienced our dialogue. She replied that she felt more comfortable and real after we laughed about my office appearing like a movie set, and she found me easy to talk to. I replied that I thought she could benefit by coming and that I would endeavor to help her become

113

better able to speak from her heart, as she put it, so that she could experience herself more authentically and that maybe some of her aesthetic sensibility would rub off on me by osmosis. She laughed and agreed to continue.

Question: What were you thinking when you presented this plan of helping her speak from her heart but then alluded to benefiting from her aesthetic sensibility?

Seinfeld: I felt that she may experience herself as inadequate because of her difficulty communicating authentically. Schizoids often do feel inept and insecure by their discomfort and difficulty in relating. Therefore, in addressing her unreal psychic state, I may have been inflicting her with a narcissistic injury. She works in the world of art and design and has a much better aesthetic sense than I. I thought it would be easier for her to hear what she was not so good at doing if I also acknowledged an area of strength. I was also saying that her area of weakness is an area of expertise and strength for me, so she should allow herself to depend on me for help. At the same time, I endeavored to circumscribe the area of dependence by indicating that there were other areas that she could know more about than I. This intervention might reduce the degree of envy that could be aroused by the patient's dependence.

Question: In your writing, you frequently describe the schizoid patient's fragmented, dissociated, and split-off states. How do you make the patient aware of these states?

Seinfeld: I can respond to this question by discussing certain issues in the case of Ellen. I was at first confused by some contradictions she presented. In this type of circumstance, I do not attempt to immediately clarify the information but rather allow myself to remain in a state of not knowing until I can reflect on what I have learned. Ellen described herself as a born-again fundamentalist Christian and ate a healthy vegetarian diet. At other times, she described herself as a postmodern disciple of critical cultural theory, a middle-aged hippie who binged on marijuana, alcohol and food, and engaged in free love. After I learned about all these different aspects of her from various incidents she had described, I did not question her about the contradictions but instead said that I was developing a picture of her based on all she had said—that she was a sex-drugs-and-rock-and-roll born-again fundamentalist right-wing Christian who lived in a postmodern left-wing relativistic hippie world. She laughed heartily and said she never quite put all those different parts of herself together. She felt like a collage of all these contradictory pieces and that each piece felt as if it were the whole of her when it is in operation.

In working with schizoid patients, it is most important that the clinician overcome the extreme detachment and apathy that can occur in both the transference and the countertransference. In the first clinical case, the patient described her life in a detached, fragmentary manner. The therapist, something of an absent-minded professor type, responded by targeting aspects of the patient's narrative, which in turn provoked the patient to feel rejected and neglected. The detachment between patient and therapist was acknowledged and analyzed. In the second clinical case, the patient manifested the schizoid defenses of depersonalization and derealization, resulting in a sense of unreality between patient and therapist. The therapist acknowledged the artificiality that is inherent in the therapeutic situation—therapy room appearing like a movie set—and the patient was able to recognize and discuss schizoid defenses.

VII

The Dynamics
of the Bad Object

The following case will elaborate on the bad object's rejection of the therapist as a potential good object. It will show how oblivion toward the therapist and acting-out behavior in the severely borderline patient can be a manifestation of the antidependent regression to the practicing subphase of separation-individuation in order to reject the vulnerable self's need for holding and rapprochement.

There will be a review of the patient's previous treatment and history, then a question-answer format will focus on the issues involved in treatment.

KIM

This case report focuses on the first three years of Kim's intensive twice-weekly treatment. Kim is a twenty-five-year-old white Irish-American. Kim was referred by a colleague after she had five years of treatment. He reported that Kim never developed a workable transference and

117

maintained a pattern of missing appointments without calling to cancel. She abused alcohol and illegal drugs at periodic intervals and did not work or attend school. The therapist was concerned about her lack of progress and inability to function. She expressed no motivation to change and used therapy sessions to boast about antisocial and destructive behavior. For instance, she boasted of tempting a friend, struggling to conquer a drug habit, into again using illegal drugs. She also engaged in behavior that threatened her own and other people's safety. Although she did not have a driver's license, she would steal her mother's car when drunk. The therapist had therefore recommended residential treatment or psychiatric hospitalization, but Kim and her mother refused.

He reported that over the first three years of treatment, he tried to engage her by understanding her worldview and empathizing with her feelings that current and past significant others failed her. He stated that although she viewed him as supportive and the only one on her side, her acting-out behavior worsened. Her attitude was "Who can blame me for messing up after all I've been through." He interpreted how she held on to a victim's position out of a fear of growing up, but to no avail. He increasingly confronted her self-destructive behavior and fear of autonomy, but she replied she had no interest in autonomy and was not concerned about her self-destructiveness. During this period, he recommended residential treatment or hospitalization and referred the case to me. He and Kim agreed that they had reached a therapeutic impasse and that she should see another therapist. He did not discontinue the treatment because he was giving up on her but rather because of his concern for her well-being and his hope that a new therapeutic experience might help her.

History

Kim was an only child in a two-parent family. Kim's mother alternately neglected and overindulged her. During Kim's first years of life, the mother often ran out of the house to escape a psychotic husband, leaving Kim in the hands of her maternal grandmother, who lived in the same apartment building. The mother promised to return later in the evening but sometimes stayed away for days at a time. Kim often awakened to find herself abandoned by the mother. She hated to fall asleep if her mother was present, and she had tantrums, insisting the mother sleep with her. During latency, she would cry unless taken to bed by the parents, and she slept with them until puberty. Her difficulty was not simply an overindulgence of dependency but rather an overindulgence following earlier neglect and abandonment. She attempted to gain omnipotent control over her parents in order to avoid the vulnerability associated with abandonment anxiety.

Kim's father had delusions that he was Jesus Christ and that demons possessed him. He underwent psychiatric hospitalization, and his condition was finally stabilized with psychotropic medication. Kim's mother went to work when she was three years old, leaving her home with her father, who was on disability. He ignored her as he read the Bible or sat in a catatonic stupor. If she disturbed him with her romping and playing, sometimes designated to get his attention, he beat her. He attempted to intimidate her with physical force, but she refused to submit and would defy him, trying never to cry. The family was always concerned that Kim resembled her father in physical appearance and that she was destined to suffer from the same psychiatric illness. When she quit high school and did not work, they

119

became unhappily convinced that she was on the same path as her father.

Throughout her childhood, Kim was on a merry-go-round in her relationships with family members. First, she would side with her mother against her father. When her mother upset her, she would go to her father. When her father upset her, she would go to her grandfather and side against everyone. When her grandfather upset her, she would go to her grandmother.

As an adolescent, Kim dropped out of school and hung out with her peers, smoking marijuana daily. She dropped out of high school at age sixteen. Her father died a year later. Kim felt indifferent about his death. She began to have paranoid episodes when she used marijuana, so she began to abuse alcohol instead.

Question: This patient fits the description of an acting-out, chaotic, disorganized borderline patient. How do you structure the treatment, provide a consisting and dependent frame, and tolerate the chaos and acting out?

Seinfeld: In simplest terms, I attempt to see such patients twice weekly on the same day and time. I am concerned that more than twice weekly with such chaotic patients could result in unmanageable regression, while less than twice weekly is not enough consistency.

Question: Do you hold to this frame unequivocally?

Seinfeld: No. This is a general frame, but there could be periods of crisis or severe depression during which the patient needs to come more often, or there could be periods when the patient begins to separate that they need to come less often. Patients who are very chaotic also may miss sessions and want makeup appointments. The therapist must use judgment as to whether the patient would best respond by the therapist holding firmly to the frame versus being flexible and rescheduling. It would be simple if there is one way that is always the right way, but unfortunately patients need different responses at different times, so the therapist cannot follow a formula but rather must use his or her autonomous judgment in assessing the needs of the patient.

In the first fifteen months of treatment, when Kim could be busy with friends, she would forget her sessions, becoming oblivious to the therapist. When I started to treat her, Kim had little structure. Her mother, who was busy working two jobs and was involved in a very active social life, would see me on occasion as a collateral but was unwilling to seek regular treatment. Kim did not sleep at night but remained awake until exhausted. Often she would sleep throughout the day, but even this was not a stable pattern. She could not tolerate being alone, and she had a set of telephone pals. She had an insomniac paraplegic friend who she could call at any hour. She enjoyed going on drinking bouts with her peers, but they were becoming somewhat less available as she grew older. Thus, she sometimes slept through her appointment time or forgot while out drinking or talking to friends on the telephone. Given the disorganization of her lifestyle, I did not see her inconsistency with appointments as only resistance but rather as a reflection of her way of life. In such instances, I suggest the therapist be as flexible as possible and agree to rescheduling within realistic parameters.

Question: How does the therapist tolerate the frustration he or she feels when faced with chaotic, out of control clients?

Seinfeld: This question is key. For the therapist to contain the client's fragmentation, the clinician must find a way to manage his or her own frustration and anger. I find it helpful to assess the patient's internal object situation and then relate this understanding to my countertransference. Kim's chief complaint is that everyone becomes busy with his own life and then abandons her. Therefore, her internal rejecting object was a busy object who put her last. The internal object was based on her actual mother, who frequently was too busy for her. Kim acted out the antidependent defense against internalizing the potential positive object therapist by identifying with the rejecting object.

In therapy and on telephone contacts, Kim recounted past and present adventures with peers. She was constantly on the run, physically and mentally. In my countertransference, I often felt my mind raced to keep up with hers. She did not seek mirroring in terms of admiration for her adventures. She usually seemed unaware of my presence, so long as she knew I was still there. On the telephone, racing through events, she might suddenly stop to make sure I was still there. She would describe her adventures in minute detail, as if she was reliving them in the telling. My position was that of a witness as opposed to an admirer. Our mode of interaction in the transference-countertransference brought to mind Mahler's practicing subphase of separation-individuation. Here I am thinking of the practicing child on the run, elated by its own physical activity and capacity, oblivious of the mother so long as it could reassure itself of her presence by returning for periodic fueling. Kim therefore demonstrated mirroring needs on the primitive, practical level of checking back for the object's continuing presence as she raced through her adventures.

In her adventures, Kim sometimes assured an invulnerable position. She could take a subway alone through two boroughs at midnight, oblivious to the concern for her safety. She would steal her mother's car and drive while drunk. In such instances, she had some degree of control (and luck) in that no harm came to her. Mahler described how the practicing child sometimes darts off, oblivious to danger, forcing the mother to give chase. In the countertransference, I often felt I had to give chase and stop Kim. Sometimes I did so by recommending psychiatric assessments, brief periods of hospitalization, or conjoint sessions with Kim and her mother. At other times I took a deep breath, let Kim go, and attempted to contain my own anxiety. As a general principle, I usually let her go and served as a witness to her adventures unless she placed herself or others at serious risk. Even so, there was often little I could do.

During all this time, throughout the first fourteen months of treatment, she seemed relatively out of contact with me. She would recount her adventures and seemed to expect nothing from me but my continued presence. She refueled by making sure I was still there after disappearing on an adventure. There was no spontaneous, gradual shift in her relatedness. She continued to miss appointments at the same rate, in much the same pattern as characterized her previous therapy. My attempts to empathize with her view of how external objects had failed her resulted in worse acting out. She used such empathy to justify her "who can blame me" attitude. Interpretations of her self-destructiveness or avoidness of individuation resulted in her increased defiance.

Question: This patient seems to be overwhelmed by any insinuation of the therapist into her life as a meaningful person. She cannot establish a workable transference, and she responds to empathy with severe self-fragmentation. Is the only option to provide her with life-management direction and to confront her self-destructiveness? What possible interventions remains?

Seinfeld: A directive or confrontational approach would likely result in further efforts at self-insulation since she is already sensitive to intrusion. The patient does have an enfeebled fragmented self as a result of trauma, as you suggest. However, it is essential to recognize that the patient actively perpetuates the trauma to protect herself from further trauma. The patient actively repeats and perpetuates the rejection she experienced to protect herself from a potential positive relationship that might later disappoint her.

Kim showed the first sign of internalizing a positive object image of the therapist by writing about me in her diary. She wrote for the first time about missing her father and wishing that she had a father like me. Her vulnerability and autonomy emerge, as she became concerned that her life was going nowhere and wished she could work or attend school. About four months into the treatment immediately following the internalization of a good object, she cut her wrist with a razor (not a suicide attempt). As she described this action, I immediately empathized with her emotional and physical pain. She looked at me scornfully and said that as she watched the blood flow, she felt invulnerable and powerful. She identified with the self doing the cutting, not the self being cut. Afterward Kim became submissive and apologetic. She pleaded with me not to drop her as a patient and agreed to a psychiatric evaluation, something she had previously refused because she did not want to be considered a "nut case" like her father.

Question: Kim tells you that she identifies with the aggressor, what you have referred to as the antidependent self identifying with the rejecting object. Is this something a therapist should focus on? If so, how?

Seinfeld: Exactly. The therapist should continually identify how the patient actively dwells on the rejecting object. Kim's mother was often too busy and preoccupied with her own problems to provide her with the attention and care she needed. Her friends were self-absorbed and related to her on a need-satisfying level. However, Kim was constantly preoccupied with how her friends and family rejected, exploited, and did not care about her. She would dwell on the rejecting object, rejected self-images throughout the day, and so remain in a victimized, depressive position. When her mother or a friend exploited her, she would fluctuate between rage and disappointment. When disappointed by her mother, she would run to her peers. When disappointed by one peer, she would run to another peer. Even when the other did not in actuality reject her, Kim interpreted the situation as a rejection. When she was away for a couple of days, she would call her mother and say, "What are you doing?" When her mother replied, "Watching television," Kim would say, "So you are too busy to speak to me," and hang up before the mother could respond. She would expect her mother to sit up all night to comfort her after she felt rejected by a boyfriend. When her mother finally said she needed to go to sleep in order to wake up early for work the next morning, Kim became enraged and depressed. She would demand her mother buy her beer and cigarettes in the middle of the night, and if the mother refused, she would accuse her of not caring and run out.

Kim became involved with a young man who was addicted to crack. He possessed the "bad" qualities of both of Kim's parents. Like her mother, he was always too busy with his friends to provide her with attention. He often stood her up if an opportunity arose to use drugs. When they did meet, he would comfort her with bottles of beer, just as her mother had given her bottles of milk in place of herself. He then took care of her, undressing her, showering her, and putting her to bed. Like her father, he was often in a drugged stupor and would experience sudden fits of rage.

Kim saw very little of this boyfriend, but she would dwell on his rejecting or exciting image all day. She would thereby elaborate on her worthlessness in relationship to his rejection. She believed he rejected her because she was not pretty enough, because she was too needy. She fantasized that he was with another girl.

The bad objects in her life were interchangeable. In dialogues with me, she discussed how her boyfriend rejected her, then switched to how her mother or friends mistreated her. In this way, she kept the bad object. Rejected self-dynamic constantly activated. Her internal bad objects resulted in narcissistic disequilibrium of depression and rage. She would therefore drink or use drugs indiscriminantly and go for a joy ride or midnight subway adventure to activate the exciting object. She then experienced elation.

During this first fourteen months of treatment, she seemed relatively out of contact with me. She recounted her adventures and disappointments and seemed to want nothing but my presence. She refueled by making sure I was still there after disappearing on an adventure.

Question: The narrative clearly illustrates how she dwelled on the rejecting object. How did you make her aware of this without conveying the sense that she was to blame for feeling everyone treated her badly?

Seinfeld: I never argued with her about reality. I empathized that the external objects often did reject her. However, her need to dwell on the feelings of rejecting was pointed out when she described a bad experience in reality. I empathized but then shifted the focus on to what she was doing in her mind with the experience. I said it was difficult to compete with crack for her boyfriend's attention. While he was off using crack, she kept him in her mind in a mode of rejection. I also pointed out how her descriptions of disappointment at the hands of her mother, boyfriend, and friends were synonymous and interchangeable. It was not difficult to show that all the external objects reflected an image—that of rejection in relation to her own image as rejected.

It was not long before she noticed that even if an experience of rejection did not occur in external reality, she would think of past rejections. She wondered why she dwelled on this rejection scenario. I replied that although she felt miserable when she activated the feelings of rejection, she held on to them because they felt safe and familiar. I said something about how feeling accepted was experienced as new, dangerous, and unwelcome. During this phase, I listened to all she said and responded from the vantage point of internalized object relations. It is best to listen to such patients as one would follow a stream of consciousness in a novel by Joyce or Proust, in which reality is always brightened or shadowed by the narrator's internal vision or experience.

Question: What kind of image does a patient so dominated by bad objects carry of the therapist? Are the bad objects split off from the transference? How does the therapist find out and respond?

Seinfeld: At some point, I ask patients about the image they usually hold of me in relationship to themselves. I usually do so after the patient is aware of the distinction between internal and external objects. If the patient is dominated by bad objects but preserves a positive sense of the therapist, I usually accept and support this because it allows the patient to remain in contact without overwhelming distress and provides the opportunity to build and strengthen a tentative and fragile internal good object. When I asked Kim about her internal relationship to me, she replied that she viewed me as caring about her and as the only person in her life who wanted her to grow into independence. I wondered why she did not maintain that image instead of always dwelling on the rejected-rejecting images. She said it was impossible for her to hold on to a sense of anyone else as caring for her when she could not care about herself. Even if she tried to hold on to a positive image of me, negative feelings about herself and others inevitably intruded and overwhelmed her.

Question: I would imagine that a patient so dominated by a bad object would experience a split-off bad object transference. If so, when and how do you deal with it?

Seinfeld: I would not interpret that patient's positive transference as a defense against the bad object. The patient may need to experience an idealizing transference to the therapist for a time. Kim defined friends as good or bad entirely on the basis of whether they spent time with her. If a friend became less available, she was easily replaced by another one. Kim originally began therapy because she was feeling alone as her friends were less available. She kept her therapy appointments when her friends were not available. Given her fear of being alone, she made friends with anyone available, and these friends often were unreliable. During sessions, she often described feeling disappointed or mistreated. As she verbalized her negative feelings about her friends, I was able to interpret her dread of being alone by remarking on how she felt forced to put up with such unreliable people because they were better than nothing. Here I did not yet focus on her beginning tendency to idealize me and view everyone else as bad objects. Instead, I began to explore how she clung to bad objects out of her fear of being alone. At this point, it was necessary to recognize her need for objects and connection because being alone evoked the dread of annihilation.

Question: How do you work with this dread of annihilation?

Seinfeld: I continually focus on the patient's abandonment dread. Kim would report that she behaved in a particular way that she imagined I did not like. She might tell me she got high or canceled a job interview. I would ask if I gave her reason to think I judged her. She was able to see that she did not like her own destructive behavior, so she believed I felt the same way. She then went into a long narrative about all the ways the boyfriend was busy and therefore left her alone. Kim did not have the capacity to be alone and therefore would have been enraged no matter what the reason. The fact that his behavior was realistically problematic gave her more of a reason to react with rage. Kim was actually showing some improvement. When she was disappointed in a boyfriend in the past, she would run out and get high, seek him out for a major fight, or act self-destructively. Now she called up numerous friends to complain of his mistreatment. Because of this small progress, I interpreted her dread of abandonment.

> *Therapist:* There is likely much reality in your statement that your boyfriend is unreliable and not treating you as a priority. This is the issue of whether he has the capacity to be a reliable boyfriend, and he may not. It may be that the intensity of your reaction is not only about this

reality situation of your relationship but also about being left alone. If you could tolerate being alone, you might find a new boyfriend or handle the situation differently. My sense is you feel it is either him or nothing.

Kim: I feel terrible. I want to get high or throw myself out of the window. I called my friends, but they were not much help.

Therapist: When you are alone, you literally feel as if you are falling apart. You feel like hurting yourself because you feel abandoned, worthless, and unlovable.

Kim: It is that way. It feels infantile, it takes over completely. I can't concentrate or read or watch a movie. I'm terrified and enraged. I don't care then about my boyfriend or myself. He's far from perfect, but sometimes he shows he cares.

Therapist: Yes, he neglects you sometimes not because you are worthless but because of his own problems. Even if he didn't care, that wouldn't be about you but about his own issues with caring.

This interpretation was long but necessary in helping her begin to distinguish internal from external objects. The patient must first have some understanding of the internal relationship before she can deal effectively with the external objects. Kim began to recall memories of being left alone, with no sense of when her mother would return. When she was jealous that her boyfriend was with others, she was reliving the feelings of abandonment when her mother left her alone for too long.

Question: How does the therapist help a patient with severe ego weakness develop the capacity to be alone?

Seinfeld: In the borderline condition, clinging is a defense against separation and abandonment depression. The above intervention illustrates this viewpoint. However, with a patient suffering from severe ego weakness, it would be unrealistic to expect them to forgo clinging dependence while becoming autonomous. A person suffering from severe pathology expresses autonomous strivings within the context of a weak and dependent ego structure. The therapist will have to support dependence that serves autonomy. As the internal separation of self and object occur, there may be clinging to external objects to alleviate separation anxiety.

Kim lived a few blocks from my office. She depended on her mother and her boyfriends to drive her to her appointment. If they were unavailable, she took a taxi. I believed that coming independently to her session meant coming on her own steam and therefore was an act of separation, so she avoided it. I did not interpret this at first because having someone take her at least enabled her to come to the sessions. However, if she could not get someone to drive her, she would miss the session. As she became attached, she would come for sessions by herself if she could not get someone to drive her and the taxi was late. She once had to walk when the taxi did not come, and she spent the first part of the session cursing her mother, her boyfriend, and the taxi. It was at this point that I interpreted that she felt abandoned when she had to come on her own. When she started looking for a job, she had her boyfriend drive her to interviews. I did not interpret this because she needed his support to begin to act autonomously. She ridiculed herself for being so immature as to need the boyfriend to drive her. I replied that even going on the interview was a sign of autonomy, that it was understandable she needed support, and that her boyfriend cared enough to provide it. She said that her experience on this job interview was different, that she was more anxious than in previous interviews. I asked why this may be, and she thought that the anxiety might imply that she was more serious about finding a job. It turned out that she did not go to work at this time. She felt like a failure and wanted to give up. I did not address my intervention around getting or not getting a job but rather explored the underlying issue of autonomy. I remarked that the fact that she experienced more anxiety was an indication of a greater wish for autonomy. I said that if she put too much pressure on herself, she could become discouraged. She said her mother would sometimes pressure her to do everything at once, and I replied that this may have been her mother's way of unconsciously discouraging her.

Question: Does the patient's fear of autonomy and abandonment emerge in the transference-countertransference situation as she begins to separate?

Seinfeld: As the patient begins to take miniscule steps at separation, there could be greater fear of being abandoned by the therapist/internal object. The patient might create a sense of despair in the transference-countertransference to assure the therapist that she will not change, that she is stuck and will need the therapist forever.

Kim sometimes expressed despair in the transference-countertransference. She said she had a terrible fight with her boyfriend; they had come to blows, and she got drunk and did not look for a job on the next day. She said there was little to live for, that she might as well be dead. No one cared. She acknowledged that I cared, but as a professional, it was part of my job. She felt helpless, that her life would never improve.

Kim's despair qualified as a negative therapeutic reaction because she was beginning to take miniscule steps at separation. She was looking more aggressively for a job, her boyfriend was free from drugs, they were living together, and she was beginning to do some household chores.

> *Kim:* I feel I'm getting nowhere now. Whenever my life shows a ray of hope, the bottom falls out. I can't get anywhere. Nothing ever helps for long.
>
> *Therapist:* You say nothing helps. You probably feel that way here as well.
>
> *Kim:* I guess we are both stuck.
>
> *Therapist:* I sense a great deal of hopelessness between us. It could be that you are attempting to communicate a feeling that we are hopelessly stuck together forever—that there is no chance there can really be any movement or change because that might threaten us with separation.

Kim was beginning to separate and individuate. One of the forms in which the negative therapeutic reaction became manifest is that she provoked her internal objects to persecute her in order to reassure herself that they still cared and did not abandon her. Fairbairn (1958) described a patient whose parents attacked her if she expressed any of her own feelings or opinions. He described a patient in the transference situation begging him to kill her and saying that if he cared about her, he would.

Kim came to sessions late, canceled without calling, and expected me to mistreat her. At times I found myself thinking of her as malingering. She also repeatedly complained of her persecutory female boss on her new job. I pointed out that up to a point, a boss was by definition a persecutor in the sense of checking that the workers come and go on time, do their work, and so forth. I said some bosses simply do the job, but others may derive a sense of sadistic satisfaction above and beyond what the position calls for. Kim felt that her boss fit that description.

133

I pointed out that her mother might also be overly controlling and the boss might stand for her mother.

Kim sometimes came in and described incidents in which she was quite provocative toward the boss. She would then complain, "The boss thinks she's the queen. Everyone treats her that way. She takes as long for lunch as she pleases. She talks on the phone and leaves early. Everyone worships her, and the company president doesn't say a word. But if I do anything like that, she is immediately on my back and tells him."

At times I found myself identified with her supervisor when she acted out resistance in therapy. Once I became so carried away in the countertransference that I said it would be understandable if the boss fired her. As a child, when Kim was disobedient, her mother had directed her father to punish her. Kim said, "My father would kill me." There was almost an undertone of pride in this statement. When I inquired about it, she said his strong reaction made her feel cared for. She endured a similar situation in the workplace as the female supervisor told the male president of the company about her disobedience. She said, "I hated her for telling him on me but then thought at least this way I came to his attention; otherwise, how would he know that I exist?"

Thus, Kim repeated the early childhood situation by telling me how badly she got along with her boss-mother and inducing me to punish her as her father had. On some level, she felt that if I lectured or attacked her, then I as the father still cared about her and was not abandoning her.

Question: How does the therapist know when the patient is ready for interpretations of splitting in the transference?

Seinfeld: The therapist must first help the patient understand the internal nature of objects. Once the patient actively understands this, the therapist can effectively interpret splitting in the transference. Kim's external object world was more bad than good in reality. Kim's mother was often too busy and preoccupied with her own problems to provide her with the attention she needed. Her friends were self-absorbed and related on a need-satisfying level. However, the internal aspect of these relationships became evident in that Kim was constantly preoccupied with how her friends and family rejected her. She would dwell on the rejecting object and rejected unimportant self-images throughout the day and thereby remain in a depressive, victimized position. Even when the external object did not necessarily reject her, Kim interpreted the situation as a rejection. When Kim was away for a couple of days, she would call her mother and ask what she was doing. When the mother replied that she was watching television, Kim would react by saying, "So you are too busy!" and hang up before the mother could respond. She expected her mother to sit up all night and comfort her when she felt rejected by a boyfriend. When the mother finally said she must get to sleep in order to wake up the next day for work, Kim would accuse her mother of not caring and run from the house. In this way, Kim contributed to the activation of the bad internal object.

Kim's running from others to peers, then from one peer to the next, recapitulated her running from one family member to another in childhood. She was on a practicing merry-go-round, always on the run but going nowhere. When running to the next object, she felt elated. Mahler stated that the elation of the practicing subphase was due not only to the exercise of the ego apparatus but also to the elated escape from merger or engulfment with the mother. By perceiving her objects as all bad and fleeing, Kim was defending against her merger needs. The flight was an antidependent rejection of the need to internalize a positive object. When Kim described the bad objects in her life, I did not argue with her about the negative qualities of her objects, but I did point out her need to dwell on the rejecting and

135

persecutory aspects of her objects. When she described a bad experience in reality, I empathized with how she felt but then shifted the focus to what she was doing in her mind to herself with that experience. It was not difficult to demonstrate how all the external objects she spoke of added up to one image of an object as rejecting and of herself as rejected.

It was not long before she noticed that even if an experience of rejection did not occur in current reality, she would dwell on past rejections. She began to wonder why she always wanted to think about herself in relation to the other as rejected. She questioned whether she might occasionally even misinterpret reality in order to conjure up the rejected feeling. I interpreted that even though she felt miserable when she activated the rejected feeling, she somehow felt safe with that feeling. I said something about feeling accepted was experienced as dangerous and unwelcome. I listened to all that she said and commented from the vantage point of her internal object relations. I listened to this patient as one would follow the stream of consciousness in a novel by Joyce or Proust, in which reality is always brightened or shaded by the narrator's internal vision and experience.

I asked the patient about the image she usually held about me in relationship to herself. She responded that she viewed me as caring about her and the only person in her life supportive of her independence. I wondered why she did not maintain that image instead of always dwelling on the rejecting and rejected images. She said it was impossible for her to hold on to the image of me or anyone else caring about her when she could not care about herself. She then reported trying to maintain positive images of herself and me but being unable to do so because the negative images and thoughts took over. As she became clear on the internal nature of her objects, I felt she was becoming ready to understand the splitting in the transference.

After she acknowledged that she could not hold on to a positive feeling in the transference, she wanted to know if I believed that her boyfriend and mother cared for her. As I explored her question, she became increasingly anxious to know my opinion. The intensity of her demand was as if she were asking if I liked her. Her certainty that I knew the answer, and the look of rejection that came over her when I did not immediately reassure her, made me feel that she was unconsciously speaking of her and me. If I were to respond in the affirmative, she would unconsciously read me to be giving her an unconscious message that I liked her. If I said no, she would unconsciously feel I was rejecting her. This type of unconscious communication in the therapeutic relationship is characteristic of the emergence of the ambivalent symbiotic phase in the therapeutic relationship.

As she complained about how her mother and boyfriend mistreated her, it was clear that she wanted something from me. She was no longer simply recounting episodes but instead wanted to know whether I saw her point of view, whether I was concerned with her plight. For the first time, she felt reassured by my empathy. I had the sense that she was unconsciously reassuring herself that I was not rejecting her. When she complained that her mother and boyfriend never called or visited her and that they did not spend enough time with her, it occurred to me that all these statements could be about me. When I pointed out that I also did not hang out with her or call her and was available only a couple of hours a week, she said that she would not expect more of me. I was a professional, the relationship was limited, and it was not appropriate for her to expect more. In this manner, she maintained a superficial therapeutic alliance with the therapist as an external object, and she split off the exciting and rejecting aspects of the transference object onto her mother and boyfriend. As I pointed out how most of her complaints about her mother and her boyfriend could apply to me, she sometimes found herself getting angry at me between sessions because she could not be with me whenever she wished. When she got drunk, she would now think of me and feel guilty. She did not like this; she felt that I made her feel guilty and controlled her mind. She therefore angrily stopped herself from thinking of me.

Question: How does the therapist manage the patient's rejecting behavior? Is interpretation the major intervention?

Seinfeld: The therapist should not be overly interpretive. The patient needs to experience the rejecting transference as a way of establishing autonomy. The unfolding of the transference will reveal the nature of the self and object configurations that are mobilized.

When I commented on her internal images, Kim became angry and complained that I sounded like a computer, that I was all intellect and had no feelings. She protested that I lacked compassion for her, that I did not care how everyone mistreated her, that I was more interested in her images than in her. She felt jealous of my interest in her images and felt that she had to compete with them for my favor. She recalled that as a child she would tell her best friend about imaginary playmates, pretending that they really existed, to make the friend jealous. When she told me of her mother, boyfriend, and friends, she realized she sometimes tried to make me jealous. She felt as if she were talking of her imaginary playmates, and when I responded to them as images, she herself became jealous. She would then ask me questions about people in my family, as if she wanted to add their images to the ambivalent symbiosis.

As she made herself jealous of my interest in her internal objects, she distanced herself from her positive image. Her jealousy was therefore the other side of the coin from her attempts to make me jealous. Kim told me that whenever the external objects did not reject her but instead expressed undeniable interest and acceptance, she herself grew cold and emotionless. The internal objects' configurations became clear. As a child, she had often felt that she and her mother continually shifted positions, one in the state of needy, insatiable, demanding child and the other cold, emotionless, distant. Kim now experienced rapid transference fluctuations of feeling schizoid detachment herself and of viewing me as needing closeness or herself as needy and I as schizoid.

Kim complained that she thought of me when she acted out and that she deliberately wanted to take in beer instead of me. She recalled that as a child, she had grown to prefer her bottle to her mother. I commented that she prefers "Bud" (Budweiser beer) to me; Bud did not expect anything of her, was always there at her command, and helped her escape her problems. She felt that I thought of myself as God-like and believed that I wanted her to put me above all others. She thought to herself, "The hell I will," and defiantly downed a bottle of beer. She sometimes perceived me as a saint and at other times as a psychotic with delusions of grandeur like her father.

At this point, at about sixteen months into her treatment, she showed a marked change in her pattern of keeping appointments. Now she rarely missed a session and was visibly upset if she was forced to be late. From this point, she started to cut down on her drinking.

Question: What relationship, if any, exists between Kim's belief that you believed yourself to be God-like and your countertransference?

Seinfeld: There is often an interactive component to transference and countertransference. Kim brought her own transferential projection in that she had a father who was sometimes subject to psychotic delusions in believing he was Christ or in communication with Christ. Therapists such as myself who have a proclivity for working with seriously disturbed patients often experience rescue fantasies. Kim came to me as a patient whom other therapists had given up on. I had my own hopes and fantasies that I would help her where others had failed her, and I would not doubt that my own competitiveness and grandiosity interacted with her transferential view that I experienced myself as a jealous god. Patients often do not project into a vacuum but rather find a characteristic in the therapist that fits the projection. Such transferential projections will be most enduring. In such instances, what might be a minor characteristic in the therapist can become considerably magnified under the enduring pressure of the projection. The above consideration is especially true in work with severely disturbed patients because of the intensity of the transference.

Q**uestion:** You described how the patient utilized a rejecting transference to establish a beginning sense of autonomy. Does the patient's projecting behavior defend against any typical underlying transference configurations? If the therapist is empathically accepting of the patient's rejecting attitude, what is likely to follow?

S**einfeld:** There is a typical sequential unfolding of the transference, although it can not be considered a cast-in-stone formula. The patient manifests a rejecting stance because he or she is threatened by any evidence that the therapist cares. If the patient experiences the therapist as caring, this may trigger a primitive exciting object transference in which the patient will wish the therapist could satisfy every one of his primitive needs. Since such an occurrence will inevitably result in frustration, leaving the patient to feel rejected, the patient rejects the therapist first to forestall the sequence of excitement/rejection.

I had referred Kim to a physician because of a minor medical problem. She came into the session enraged at the physician's nurse. She had attempted to persuade the nurse to allow her to go in before other patients because she had an appointment with me afterward and did not want to be late. The nurse had not permitted it but did try to comfort and calm her. Kim stormed out, accusing the nurse of infantilizing her. She angrily complained to me about the nurse and the physician and then grew fearful of me that I was angry at her for criticizing the referral. She was angry at me for sending her to someone else but then projectively identified her own anger into me and imagined herself as rejected.

That night, still quite fearful that I was angry at her, she had two dreams. In the first, her current boyfriend became a homosexual and no longer liked her. In the second dream, she received repeated crank calls. I was the caller but identified myself as someone else. She recognized my voice and knew it to be me and was frightened that this meant I was psychotic like her father. She had always called me when she was upset, but now she felt terribly alone. She could not call me because I was the one with whom she had a problem.

Her immediate association to the dream was that it was easier to talk to me about her boyfriend going crazy than it was for her to acknowledge her unconscious belief that I was crazy. She remembered that she had called me a year earlier to say that she believed her boyfriend was making crank calls, pretending that he was someone else to see if she was home, then she received some sexually provocative calls when he was angry at her, so she believed it was he or his friends. Now she could see that the boyfriend and I were one and the same to her unconsciously. In the dream, she continually thought, "I know he's not someone else; I know he is my therapist." What she thought the dream meant is that she knew the crazy object image was not the boyfriend, but she pretended that it was because if she allowed herself to think that I was crazy, to mistrust my motives, or to feel that I was like her father, then she would be all alone. Whom could she tell? Her mother, her boyfriend, her friends? It was much easier to tell me that she feared I was crazy and that she had crazy feelings about me if she disguised me in the image of her boyfriend.

Kim's image of me as caring for her was strengthened when I responded to her request to help her find a physician. She therefore activated the all-bad self and object transference configuration by rejecting the referral and rejecting me in retaliation. When she saw me as caring for her, she was threatened by her own libidinal needs and by the arousal of the exciting object transference. She therefore dreamt that the boyfriend, who represented the therapist unconsciously, was not interested in her libidinally. This dream denied the unconscious wish for the therapist to be the exciting object who was interested in her libidinally. The second dream made it apparent that she had been splitting off the exciting and rejecting aspects of the transference onto the crazy, exciting, rejecting boyfriend.

Following these dreams, she experienced the ambivalent symbiosis directly in the transference. After a weekend, she would come in for a session and say that she believed I was angry at her and no longer liked her. She then felt angry at me and no longer liked me. Once she said, "The hell with him," and had gotten drunk. When her reasons for feeling I had rejected her were explored, it became apparent that she had become angry because the weekend meant she had finished her weekly sessions and could no longer see me. She felt angry and rejected and projectively identified her anger onto me.

Kim now perceived me as rejecting her in much the same manner that she had previously felt rejected by her mother and boyfriend. If she called and I was not immediately available to speak to her, she complained that I was always busy, always put her last, and did not care about her. When we did speak by telephone, she inevitably felt rejected because at some point I would say that I had to end the conversation. She herself would never end the dialogue and would feel rejected when I had to go, regardless of how long our conversation had been. She believed that I preferred my other patients, that I considered her my craziest patient. She complained that I was always too busy, just like her mother, and imagined that I gave her more attention when she was acting out in some way. Now that she had become more autonomous and acted out less, I was becoming busier in my own life and would abandon her as everyone else had.

At times she could briefly maintain a positive image of herself and me, but the negative thoughts of herself rejected by me would predominate. She would tell herself that she would no longer care about me. She felt that I betrayed her by allowing her to depend on me and by telling her it was self-destructive to depend on alcohol. She felt that I had encouraged her to depend on me but then left her with only an image to depend on. She wondered how that was supposed to help her. She needed me— the real external object to be available whenever she needed me. She would angrily reject the positive image of herself and me but then feel depressed and alone and have to reconnect to reconstitute her positive self and object representations. She now experienced rapid fluctuations of negative and positive self and object images in the transference, but the negative ones continued to dominate.

Question: How might different psychodynamic schools understand this patient's transference manifestations? How do these views relate to your own understanding?

Seinfeld: I think the American object relations school would view Kim's insatiable object need as an attempt to establish the rewarding object relations unit to avoid abandonment depression. The depression and rage she experienced would be viewed as the inevitable outcome of disappointment in the rewarding object. The technical management of the case, from this perspective, would involve the confrontation of the patient with the reality that dependence on the rewarding object must inevitably result in disappointment and frustration. The patient must relinquish the fantasy of the all-good object and face the abandonment depression.

The American school of object relations describes the splitting of the object in borderline patients as between a rewarding (of infantile dependency) object and a rejecting object. The rewarding object is inevitably mobilized to defend against abandonment depression. The American object relations theory's conception of the rewarding object is quite comparable to the British object relations exciting object. In both schools, the object excites intense, insatiable libidinal need. The American school designates this self and object relations configuration as the rewarding object relations unit, the British school as the libidinal ego-exciting object. In my view, the insatiable need experienced in this object relations configuration serves the antidependent defense. By making her need for contact with the exciting or rewarding object insatiable, the patient can perceive of herself as rejected regardless of the external object's behavior. Therefore, the patient is always able to think of her needs as being unmet, to think of herself as worthless and rejected and of the object as rejecting. The activation of the rejecting self and object relations unit results in rage and depression. The insatiable need of the oral self-exciting object unit is then activated to defend against abandonment depression as described by the American school. In this regard, the all-bad self and object relations unit becomes a vicious cycle constituting both the exciting and the rejecting objects. In my view, the patient activates both of these bad object relations configurations to defend against the internalization of the positive self and object unit.

Self psychology understands and effectively describes how insatiable need can serve to compensate for the depression and rage of the fragmented self. However, it is my sense that self psychology neglects the point that insatiable need also serves to maintain the perception of the object as rejecting in antidependent defense. This patient succinctly stated the antidependent position, "If I think you do not like me, why should I bother to like you?"

When the patient is caught in the vicious exciting and rejecting cycle, it is necessary to interpret the antidependent defense. In this way, the patient can eventually maintain the positive self and object relations transference, and the ambivalent symbiosis can evolve into a therapeutic symbiosis. I continually commented on how Kim focused on all the ways I was not available because this was safer than focusing on the way in which I was potentially available. It is important to first accept the patient's anger at feeling abandoned before interpreting this as a defense so that the patient does not feel the clinician is simply talking the patient out of her anger. As Kim increasingly noticed her rejection of internal positive self and object images, she also noted that she often alienated external objects through rejecting and demanding behavior. She realized that if she was not provocative, external objects were not always bad and that even her mother, on occasion, had a positive side.

Question: What does the patient fear in the activation of the positive transference? You seem to be describing this as the core or primary anxiety underlying the vicious cycle of the exciting and rejecting objects. What occurs as the patient internalizes the therapist as a positive or potentially good object?

Seinfeld: The patient's primary fear is the awakening of vulnerability. As Kim began to feel vulnerable to me and in her current life situation, she was astonished that she had taken midnight subway rides and indulged in drunken sprees. She felt that she had made herself vulnerable and realized that when the all-bad view of images dominated her, she felt depressed and enraged but also less vulnerable. She said that sometimes when she was out of control, she experienced a sense of power in forcing others to control her. She had been similar to a child in the practicing subphase who darts off into danger and forces the mother to chase and catch her.

She became aware of her inability to take care of herself and began to think of school and work. When such patients do not function, they often deny their fear of not knowing and their vulnerability. There is a certain infantile omnipotence in their passive dependence. To admit that one has something to learn, to initially experience the phase of learning and uncertainty that occurs prior to achieving mastery, requires accepting one's vulnerability and lack of omnipotence. By doing nothing, Kim could feel that she had nothing to learn. She could insist on always being right and could avoid the narcissistic injury of having to learn and depend on the other for help. It was not difficult to understand the genesis of her denial of vulnerability. Whenever Kim had tried to learn anything, her mother and father were highly critical of her beginning fumbling and imperfections. By attacking her vulnerability in the beginning phase of learning, they also indirectly affected her strivings for autonomy. Kim could therefore never admit not knowing and could never experience the initial learning process because the internal object rejected this vulnerability. In school, she did not permit herself to learn but instead sat apathetically until she quit at sixteen. She could also not admit the vulnerability to learning on a job.

As she entered rapprochement and experienced the wholesale rejection of her autonomy and vulnerability, she fled back to the practicing phase, from which she could at least experience some self-esteem. In this way, she denied the vulnerable self's need for the internal holding object. Instead, she made the object all bad and fled into omnipotence.

The vulnerable self became connected to the holding object in the transference. It was at this point that she experienced the core anxieties. She experienced severe separation anxiety. She faced the fact that her life was a mess and that she felt like a vulnerable child. She began to believe that I was really going to help her, that our relationship could affect the rest of her life. She therefore feared what would become of her if something were to happen to me. She was experiencing the vulnerability of the rapprochement child when she discovers her separateness and dependence on the object.

She recalled that as a child she had not experienced separation reactions when she began nursery for a full day. She remembered the other children crying for their mothers and thinking that they were babies. She felt only elation about starting school. She recalled that the children were not allowed to play the piano during the rest period and that she felt this was unfair. She repeatedly ran to the piano to play, and the teacher angrily stopped her. When Kim told her mother of the problem, the mother pulled her from the school. Kim now wondered whether she had been actually covering up her separation anxiety and vulnerability by acting out her omnipotence and doing whatever she pleased.

Kim began to feel vulnerable in relationship to me. She had thoughts that I could physically overpower and rape her. Although she did not rationally think of me as a rapist, she would sometimes feel for a fleeting moment that if I was crazy I could rape her. She realized she was thinking not only rape in a physical sense but also my somehow mentally raping or overpowering her. She recalled at times thinking of her father as a psychotic rapist. She wondered whether she had not defied him out of fear that if she showed her vulnerability, he would rape her physically and mentally.

She had a dream that she had admitted a man to her house who looked like me; the man had been psychotic and raped her. The fear reflected that if she let me in her mind as an internal object, I would overpower and dominate her sense of self. In addition, the wish for comfort and protection from the internal object promoted the wish to internalize the object through a primitive sexualized and aggressive mode. She therefore thought of internalizing the object in a physical, sexualized sense through a rape fantasy. Her father's psychosis certainly complicated whatever sexualized fantasies she had about him.

As she increasingly accepted her vulnerable need for the internal holding object, she reported beginning to feel self-empathy. She felt sorrow for the lonely and vulnerable child she had been. She then criticized herself for feeling sorry for herself. She said that in the past she had always felt victimized and rejected and had tried to make others feel sorry for her so that she could control them, but she had never felt sorry for herself. Kim now began to manifest a therapeutic symbiosis.

She bought a parrot to keep her company. She would joke that the bird was a good listener and kept her company when I was not around. The bird was a transitional object of the therapist reinforcing the internal positive image. Sometimes, the bird represented her vulnerable self; she wanted to be a mother to the bird and care for it and was very aware of the fact that the bird's life was in her hands. Sometimes, despite her efforts, she became preoccupied with bad self and object images. She would ignore the bird, forgetting its vulnerability and its existence. The bird would become noisy, get into things, and distract her. Kim would become enraged, scream, and chase the parrot. She would then feel like the "bad mother." She felt empathy for her own mother, realizing the difficulty of devoting oneself to another. When she cared for the bird, she thought of it as a good object, always available. She imagined the bird was grateful and loved her. She felt that she was a good mother and the bird a good child, but she simultaneously felt that the bird was a good mother mirroring her for being a good child. When she was neglecting the bird, she imagined that it hated and rejected her. She simultaneously felt that she was the bad rejecting mother to the unworthy child and that the bird was a bad rejecting mother hating her as an unworthy child. The patient's symbiotic relatedness to the bird reflected the growing therapeutic symbiosis in the transference.

Her relationship to the bird and to the external therapist reinforced her positive internal image of the therapist. Gradually, the good object gained dominance over the bad object. At this point, she split off the negative unit onto the insensitive external world and felt protected by the symbiosis. Therefore, although she continued to view the external world as all bad, she was less sensitive to impingement from that world in that the therapist's empathy comforted her. Disrupting of the therapeutic symbiosis now came not so much from her side of the therapeutic field as from occasional empathic failures by the therapist. Once when I was tired during a session, my mind wandered from what she had said, and my response revealed that I had misunderstood her. She went into a rage, accused me of sleeping on the job, of being incompetent, of not taking care of her. Her rage was quickly calmed as I abruptly awakened from my therapeutic lethargy and gave her my undivided attention. The therapist's occasional non-traumatic failures resulted in increasing integration of good and bad internal objects.

As Kim became less depressed and angry, her vulnerability and strivings for autonomy increasingly emerged. Having decided she must do something to change her life, she managed to get a high school equivalency diploma and began college. In the transference evolution, she became somewhat disillusioned with the therapist as the mother transference object who discouraged autonomy and encouraged dependence. As she separated in the transference, she brought to the therapist her ambitions and interests for mirroring admiration. Her ambitions, which initially were grandiose, started to become more realistic.

Question: What is the major anxiety motivating the antidependent retreat from internalization of the object?

Seinfeld: The core issue is the fear that the object will take over and control the mind. The fear of mind control expresses through the internal object relations situation the identical interpersonal concept of merger anxiety.

At the height of her acting out, she denied her human vulnerability and once said that she wanted to make someone stop her but also that she would not let anyone. Because of the patient's own lack of internal structure and sense of being out of control, she craves an object to take in to provide structure and control but also fears losing her mind and identity to the object. She therefore makes the object all bad to avoid the temptation to internalize a seemingly positive object that could become bad through mind control, and so she rejects the internalization of the good object through practicing flight and thereby plays out the need for control sadomasochistically by challenging the external object to control her externally and behaviorally. Acting out then becomes a means of shifting the conflict about control from the internal to the external behavior sphere. The conflict of "will I or will I not let you in?" shifts to the safer ground of "can you or can you not control me from the outside?"

150

A patient expressed this aptly: "I'd like my body to be controlled by someone else. When someone dominates me from the
outside, I feel in control of both myself and them. I no longer
feel inside of me but can feel myself outside of my body, as if I
joined them in controlling me. I have therefore turned the tables
in my mind and feel in control of them and of myself. What I hate
is when I feel someone could get in my mind, when I feel they
could put thoughts into me, influence my thoughts, or take
thoughts out of me. Then I feel they can control my mind."

VIII

The Negative
Therapeutic Reaction
in the Treatment of Children

This chapter will describe how the therapist can serve as a developmental self-object in the treatment of severely disturbed children. Such children are manifesting practicing subphase behavior and a paranoid-schizoid level of object relations. I will illustrate how child therapy has developed from an ego-supportive impulse psychology orientation to one based on self and object relations theory. Clinical vignettes will be utilized to illustrate how the child's disordered, chaotic, destructive behavior serves the bad object's rejection of a holding therapeutic relationship and how practice implications of self and object relations theory in some ways differ from classical ego-supportive methods.

Question: What were the early principles of child therapy?

Seinfeld: Melanie Klein and Anna Freud were the originators of child therapy, within a classical impulse psychology perspective.

This model suggests that the child suffers from unconscious guilt because of instinctual impulses not acceptable to the reality principle or the superego. This symbolic expression of these impulses through the play technique and through verbalization freed the child from infantile neurosis. The instinctual impulses could find expression in a manner acceptable to the ego, which served as a mediator between id, reality, and superego. Freud and Klein diverged on questions of technique. Freud developed a preparatory method based on guidance, education, and support to strengthen the ego and superego in order to ensure that the child did not act on impulses emerging from repression. Freud's preparatory technique involved the strengthening of character so that the child was not corrupted by the uncovering of the id or the expression of instinctual derivatives. Klein disagreed with Freud about the need for a preparatory phase of ego building and instead directly interpreted the id and the transference. Despite differences in technique, Freud and Klein developed their pioneering techniques from a classical perspective.

In the course of the history of child therapy in the United States, children were increasingly viewed as having difficulty repressing, as opposed to expressing, instinctual impulses. Freud's ego-supportive preparatory model served as a framework for an ego-supportive psychotherapeutic approach that replaced classical analysis as the treatment of choice. The view of the child patient as suffering from unconscious guilt, repression, and infantile neurosis was gradually supplemented in the treatment setting by the conduct disordered or borderline youngster viewed as experiencing problems of impulse control, ego weakness, poor judgment, and superego deficiency. Ego-supportive techniques included suggestion, abreaction, manipulation, clarification, reassurance, and corrective emotional experience with a new object. The emphasis shifted to viewing such youngsters as experiencing deficits in early object relations. The parental figure did not provide the child, in early development, with sufficient structure, limits, and support that would build strong ego defenses and functions to serve the ego as a bulwark against the id. In ego-supportive treatment, the therapist was viewed as lending a strong auxiliary ego to the patient's weak, chaotic ego. The therapist provided boundaries, limits, and structure in response to disorganized, impulsive behavior. The ego-supportive method remained within a classical perspective in that the focus was still on instinctual impulses but with a shift in emphasis from uncovering to suppression or repression of impulses.

Question: What are some examples of ego-supportive techniques?

Seinfeld: In order to illustrate how the clinical working from a classical impulse psychology perspective might intervene with ego-supportive techniques, let us consider the typical problem of a child who cheats in a game with the therapist.

If the child is believed to be at the neurotic oedipal level of development, cheating might be met with an interpretative intervention. It would be interpreted to the child in terms of a forbidden oedipal triumph and as unconscious guilt within a wish to be caught or punished.

If the child is viewed as expressing a belief in the omnipotence of instinctual impulse, a predominance of the pleasure over the reality principal, limits may be set on cheating. The therapist might then empathically encourage the child to verbalize his disappointment, frustration, anger, or sadness over the loss of infantile omnipotent impulse gratification. The therapist would thereby attempt to strengthen the conduct-disordered child's ego functions of impulse control, judgment, and frustration tolerance by directing him away from the real action toward that of verbalization.

If the child is viewed predominantly as suffering from a narcissistic disorder and is considered to have fragile self-esteem, the therapist might limit the cheating but provide the child with a handicap or advantage to compensate for the inequality in ability. The therapist thereby limits omnipotence but also communicates empathy for the child's poor self-worth. If the child is viewed as severely borderline and if his ego is so disorganized and unstructured that he is unable to learn the rules of the game and he plays randomly and chaotically, the therapist might allow the child to make up the rules but then attempt to add some consistency and structure to the child's play.

Question: How does self and object relations theory approach such approaches of intervention?

Seinfeld: The assumption that the youngster is cheating involves a belief on the therapist's part that the child and therapist are playing in the realm of instinctual gratification and competition. The therapist believes the child is omnipotently cheating a reality or morality perspective that child and therapist share. The oedipal competitive dimension becomes the ideal that the child cheats, denies, and omnipotently repudiates.

Recent advances in self and object relations theory have raised questions about the reality and morality domain of classical impulse psychology. These theories do not always view omnipotence in terms of unrestricted instinctual gratification and the dominance of the pleasure over the reality principle.

Edith Jacobson and Margaret Mahler have emphasized the importance and value of a very early period of omnipotent fusion between infant and mother, a symbiotic phase only gradually relinquished in a prolonged process of separation individuation.

Kohut speaks of a sense of narcissistic omnipotence invested in the parental figure as self-object that is gradually relinquished through the transmuting internalization of the self-object. Winnicott speaks of the true self seeking, through the omnipotent gesture, the acceptance of the holding object. Despite differences in these self and object relations theories, they have all professed that an early phase of omnipotent fusion between infant and mother is the foundation of the development of an authentic, constant sense of autonomous self.

The therapeutic implications of this idea are significant. The therapist, in relating to patients who suffer primitive mental states, will attempt to serve as an extension of the patient's self, as a developmental self-object. In self and object relations theory, the therapeutic process is shifting into the realm of mirroring, holding, and idealizing as opposed to provision of direction, education, manipulation, and limits.

In the therapeutic process that I describe, the child's chaotic activity embodies primitive psychic structures that become mobilized through the self, self-object transference, promoting higher levels of structuralization and ego functioning. If the therapist attempts to provide too much in the way of active, ego-supportive measures, he may inadvertently interfere with the structuralization that can emerge from chaotic activity. From this point of view, the therapist serves as an extension of the child's self instead of imposing his separate self on the patient's self or his strong auxiliary ego on the patient's weak ego by providing external boundaries and structures.

Question: How does the negative therapeutic reaction manifest in children? How does one recognize the children susceptible to this reaction?

Seinfeld: The children to whom these views may be applied are extremely disturbed in a very specific sense. These children behave as if the ordinary rules and structures in everyday life are an affront to their sense of omnipotence. They are often described as wanting to do whatever they wish whenever they wish. Any instruction in any realm whatsoever is regarded as a narcissistic injury. Such children are often described as extremely hyperactive, learning disordered, undersocialized, and severely conduct disordered. In their defiance, they often endanger themselves or others. They seem oblivious to others, and they reject help and empathy; the provision of help is also seen as a narcissistic injury to their sense of omnipotence. These children cannot accept the hesitancies of learning, of not knowing, and they insist they know all. They resemble a cat chasing its own tail; their frenzied activity is chaotic and leads to little visible accomplishment. Efforts to control them are met with temper tantrums. If they are finally restrained or limited, they make no good use of such restraint but instead become apathetic and uninterested.

These youngsters often come from family systems in which the parents are harshly critical of their efforts to learn. The parents are often overbearing or engulfing; they see the child as an extension or self-object of themselves rather than permitting the child to relate to them as an extension of the child's self. The child is likely to be harshly rejected or abused if he presents a vulnerable or dependent self to the parental objects for holding or comfort. The child will also be rejected if he rejects the parents' self-object needs for him. The parents' engulfing behavior results in the child becoming overly sensitive to any efforts at control or structure. In an effort to experience some sense of omnipotent control, the child reverts to practicing subphase behavior. He acts as if he is oblivious to the human external object world. As he runs about, he experiences others as obstacles or as engulfing or controlling. At the same time, the child will get into trouble and thereby force the objects to chase after him. The practicing subphase behaviors can be used by the child to flee from an engulfing image of a parent.

In the treatment situation, these youngsters often reject empathy, mirroring, and limit setting by the therapist. Any sign or progress or connection with the therapist is immediately undone by a negative therapeutic reaction manifested by increasing acting out and destructive behavior. The following two clinical vignettes illustrate the dynamics of the negative therapeutic reaction and the ways the therapist may intervene.

ROBERT

Robert was a nine-year-old Latino youngster referred for treatment because of severe hyperactivity and aggressive behavior. School officials reported that he was out of control, behaved aggressively with other children, and did not follow any of the teacher's instructions. Despite the fact that he attended a small, structured classroom for emotionally disturbed children, he did not respond to limit setting or nurturing help; according to the principal, he was in need of medication or a structured, authoritative, behavioral management type of residential program or both.

Robert responded negatively to help, nurturance, or praise. If he was finally forced to sit still, he became withdrawn and sullen and just waited for the restraint to be lifted. When his parents or teachers criticized him, he sometimes spoke of wanting to die. He had once made a suicidal gesture by tying a rope around his neck and saying that he was going to hang himself.

Robert, the only child of divorced parents, lived with his mother and visited his father irregularly. His parents could be severely critical of anything he wanted to do. His mother would ask him to do a chore but then criticize him and take over the task herself. He internalized this rejection of his autonomy and thereby rejected whatever he drew or built. He would draw a picture, become dissatisfied with some imperfection, and destroy the picture. Robert stopped trying to learn and instead insisted that he already knew. In this way, he avoided the vulnerability associated with not knowing and learning and assumed an omnipotent position of knowing everything and trying nothing.

Robert's parents often turned to him as a self-object or transitional object, treating him as an extension of themselves instead of allowing him to experience them as self-objects. Robert's father never called him but complained that Robert never called. When the boy appeared in a school play, Robert's father did not come and complained that Robert invited his mother and not him, although Robert had not extended a special invitation to his mother. His mother did not hug or display affection to her son but complained that Robert did not kiss her. She would approach him before he left the house and say, "give me a kiss," and he would turn away. Robert experienced his parents' self-object needs for him as engulfing and attempted to flee through his hyperactive, frantic activity.

Question: How does the clinician attempt to engage a youngster such as Robert in the treatment process? Is this similar to or different from the usual method of engagement in child therapy?

Seinfeld: Generally, I have on the play table several objects that can be used for symbolic play. These might include a family of dolls, a doll house, puppets, toy soldiers, playing cards, and drawing paper with crayons or paint. I might ask the child questions about where he or she lives, where he or she goes to school, who are his or her best friends and enemies, and what are his or her favorite television show, movies, or food or to describe a best and worst teacher. I allow the child to select the object to play with as well as how to play with it.

Robert did not play with the materials in a symbolic or sublimated fashion. Instead, he tried to destroy them, pulling the dolls apart, aimlessly throwing them and distractedly shifting from one activity to the next. Any attempt to question him in an innocuous way was futile. He ignored questions and became increasingly destructive and aggressive.

I generally "hang out" with such children and intervene only when they are about to destroy something. For instance, as Robert was pulling a doll apart, I said in a low tone, "Not so hard." I did not explain that the toys in the room are to be played with but not destroyed, nor did I say he could not break things or hurt himself or me. I have found that such speeches either exacerbate the severely disturbed child's acting out or provoke sullen withdrawal. I therefore keep such comments to the bare minimum, communicating only the most essential words because I want to limit the child's destruction while still permitting him to bring the stormy behavioral problems into the session.

When Robert would destroy his drawings, I attempted to neither save his pictures nor influence his perceptions of them. The child who destroys all his work as unworthy has activated the internal rejecting object, the pictures representing his own rejected self. If the therapist attempts to align himself prematurely with the rejected self, the rejecting behavior will become exacerbated. Robert was rejecting his vulnerable self's need for a helping object. His rejecting behavior was the opposite type of behavior from that of the child who draws a picture and hopes for the object's admiration or approval. As Robert threw away his drawing, I intervened by hanging around and not doing anything. This is an intervention because it accepts his need to identify with the rejecting object and permits him to relate to me in a rejecting, antidependent manner. The therapist often intervenes with borderline children through action and behavior instead of words.

In the first few sessions, no attempt was made to contact Robert except for the initial innocuous introduction. He became increasingly wild and aggressive. At one point, he aimlessly threw a rubber ball around the room and accidentally hit and broke a picture on the wall. He waited for my reaction, and I wordlessly cleaned up the broken glass and said nothing about breaking any more pictures. When he later wildly threw the ball in the direction of the pictures, I simply said, "Not so near." He then made a concerted effort to aim away from the pictures. When he threw again in the direction of the pictures, I said, "Not so near." A few throws later, he again threw in the direction of the pictures, and I saw him catch himself as if to say, "Oh, I forgot." I believe this catching of himself was the first sign that he had begun to internalize me, so I did not say, "Not so near," thinking that he would hear this remark as engulfing since he had already said it to himself. I was confirmed in this view by the fact that the next time he threw the ball, he aimed far away from the pictures.

Question: How would you compare this approach to the traditional ego-supportive approach? How would you distinguish which approach would be more effective in a specific clinical situation?

Seinfeld: With the ego-supportive approach, the therapist would be more active in setting limits and providing structure for instance by informing the youngster that he cannot throw the ball aimlessly or by setting up a target or object at which the child can take aim. The therapist introduces reality, boundaries, and structure in the sense that the therapist tries to lend a strong ego to the child's weak ego. With a child whose psychic structure is as undeveloped as Robert's, there is a clear danger that the youngster will experience such ego support as engulfing. The child becomes initially antilibidinally aggressive and withdraws if the therapist succeeds in restraining him. The approach I describe with Robert attempts to achieve a difficult balance. The therapist provides limits but minimally and in such a way that the child internalizes them instead of rejecting them as engulfing. The therapist endeavors to gently catalyze the child into building his own psychic structure instead of borrowing the therapist's psychic structure. I find egosupportive techniques useful for children who have established significant psychic structure but are temporarily regressing or resistant.

Robert made his first direct contact with me by throwing the ball at me. I caught it and waited. He called me "stupid" and said I should throw it back, and I did. We engaged in our first game of catch as Robert's transference shifted from the out-of-control to the ambivalent symbiotic phase. Robert instructed me on how to throw and catch the ball. I tried to follow his instructions but could never do it well enough for him. He talked to me for the first time. "You didn't do it right. Throw it from the side. No, make it curve. Too straight. That's not right. Watch me. What's the matter with you? Were you watching? Are you a retard? Do it right."

I did not respond verbally but followed his instructions the best I could. His verbal abuse continued, and he blamed me if I threw the ball and he dropped it.

In the transference, he identified with the rejecting object and projected into me his inadequate, vulnerable self. He abused me as his parents abused him. The antilibidinal stance was now fully activated in the transference situation. He threatened me with abandonment, saying, "If you don't do it right, I'm not coming back."

He directed me to retrieve the ball, to pick it up from the floor, to move furniture out of the way to clear our field of catch. Sometimes he referred to me as "slave" and "servant." I followed his instructions silently.

After a time, the game of catch became quite elaborate. He did tricks with the ball before throwing it. He would throw it three times over an outstretched arm, catching it with his other hand, then throw it behind his back from one hand to the next and repeat the throws with the other arm outstretched. He could barely do this juggling act; the ball kept dropping or he would forget the next step in the sequence. But then he would expect me to do the same trick after watching his fumbling efforts once. If I dropped the ball or did not follow the sequence exactly, he would become enraged and accuse me of being inattentive and stupid, demanding that I return the ball to him so that he could further instruct me. I had to pay close attention to follow the trick, and once I got it right, he would tell me I was mistaken and add another step to the trick. He never allowed me to practice anything that I learned, and he set up the situation so that I repeatedly failed. This pattern of interaction went on for one year.

Question: Could you describe how the therapist comes to recognize through the transference-countertransference enactment the early parent-child interaction?

Seinfeld: The patient and therapist often drive each other crazy in a mode that reenacts how the patient as a child and the parent drove each other crazy and then therapist and patient endeavor to overcome this pattern as the parent and child had been unable to.

In the treatment of Robert, our pattern began to shift. For prolonged periods, he would engage me in a game of catch during which we would throw the ball as straight as possible to each other. This catch would go on for the entire session, session after session. Sometimes it was very relaxing, and I felt as if I were in a reverie or a trance. It could be almost hypnotic. At other times it became monotonous, my mind would wander, and I, not fully concentrating, would not catch or throw exactly as Robert wanted. In such instances, he would scream that I was not paying attention, that I must concentrate, that he would make the rules of the game more difficult so that I had to give it my undivided attention. I sometimes found my mind wandering even though I had made up my mind to give it my fullest attention. It was as if a form of splitting occurred and part of my mind rebelled against his demand that I fully concentrate on our interaction.

The transference-countertransference relatedness indicated the evolution of a fully activated ambivalent symbiosis. Robert was, on the other hand, the mother demanding the full attention of the child. When he felt that he had lost control of my mind in our interacting, he would become rejecting and abusing in much the same manner that his parents had abused him when his mind wandered outside their orbit. On the other hand, he was simultaneously the child demanding that his schizoid, detached mother provide him with her full attention.

I met with Robert's mother regularly on a child guidance basis and knew her to be extremely absentminded, "in the clouds," and self-preoccupied. In fact, she spontaneously reported that she often felt that she walked around in a trance and was out of touch with everyday happenings around her. She was so preoccupied that she often would not hear Robert when he asked a question. He set up this monotonous game of catch, which eventually induced within me the schizoid drifting of the mother. This interaction actually repeated the ambivalent symbiotic relatedness between him and his mother. In Robert's early childhood, his mother often demanded his full attention and tried to control his every thought. At the same time, when he demanded her attention, she would drift off mentally in schizoid detachment. Her efforts to control his thoughts and attention in turn provoked him into mind-wandering distraction and schizoid unrelatedness to flee from her mental engulfment. She had demanded that he concentrate on her, but she wandered off mentally when he tried to get her to concentrate on him. I came to believe that much of his distractibility and hyperactivity reflected his internal efforts to flee from the engulfing object that was demanding his full attention. In school, he was notoriously known for paying no attention to instructions, shifting from one activity to the next, and being in his own world. In our sessions, he attempted to correct the pathological ambivalent symbiosis by omnipotently controlling my attention and demanding that I not mentally wander off in schizoid detachment. At the same time, he re-created an irrational atmosphere (the monotonous game of catch) that would induce my mind to wander in schizoid detachment.

The ambivalent symbiosis was at a peak of intensity when Robert finally ended our game of catch and instructed me to do physical exercise. He commanded that I do army push-ups, which involved clapping one's hands as one pushed oneself up and down. He ordered me to do fifty, and I did as many as I could without straining myself. He called me weak and a sissy and instructed me to do one hundred sit-ups. After I rested, with Robert telling me to stop being lazy, I did sit-ups without straining myself. Robert said I was not so tired and could do more. I rested for a while and did a few more, then rested again while he called me lazy and weak. He then ordered me to do a one-arm push-up. Had I attempted such a push-up, I would have fallen flat on my face. However, I got into the position to demonstrate that it was not possible. He insisted that I do it and then picked up a pencil and said he would break it if I did not do the push-up. When I did not reply, he said he would break the pencil by the count of ten. "One, two, three, four," he said and added, "Should I break it? If you don't tell me not to break it I will . . . five, six, seven . . . tell me to break it or not to break it, eight, nine . . . you'd better tell me. If you don't say anything I'll break it. Come on . . . ten. Should I break it? I'm not kidding, say something." He placed the pencil on the desk unbroken and said rather meekly that he was just kidding, adding, "See, I didn't break it."

I was surprised that he seemed concerned that I recognize that he did not break the pencil. This was the first instance in which my reaction seemed to matter to him. I felt certain that if I told him to either break or not break the pencil, he would have broken it. The exchange between us demonstrates the need to help the child to find his own limits to his destructive behavior. Our interaction also inaugurated the therapeutic symbiotic phase of the transference evolution.

In our next session, Robert again instructed me to do army push-ups. Again, I did as many as I could. He applauded and said I was terrific. He then told me to do the same number of sit-ups that I had done last time. He applauded, and for the first time he positioned himself to do push-ups. He then looked at me for my reaction and said, "That wasn't good. Not as many as you do." I said, "You did fine."

In our future interactions, he would sometimes begin to scold me for not doing something right or quickly enough but then would become concerned that he had hurt my feelings and add that he did not mean it. In this way, he began to develop a capacity for concern for the object. He became interested in doing the tricks with the ball himself during our catch play instead of instructing me on how to do them. He would now say I did not do it right and let me practice. I would "hang around" and just watch without commenting on his efforts unless he asked directly. Then I would say, "You did fine." He now seemed able to take in such succinct, positive comments. He began to take pride in how well he and I did exercises, played catch, and so on. On such occasions, the all-good self and object unit was in ascendance, and he and I were the best of teams. This play activity is equivalent to the symbiotic phase described earlier, in which the adult patient feels that he and the therapist are the best of therapeutic teams. At other times, when he criticized himself or me, the all-bad self and object unit dominated this phase of therapeutic symbiotic transference.

Question: What was the change in his internal object relations that was reflected in his change of behavior in sessions?

Seinfeld: His efforts to do exercises and tricks, with the admission that he did not do them well, and the acceptance of his fumblings in learning meant that the vulnerable true self was emerging in the transference in relation to the holding object. The spontaneous true self was manifested in his feelings and expressions of disappointment and joy as he practiced tricks and exercises. It was fascinating to watch the transformation as the abusive and omnipotent behavior gave way to the natural behavior of a child. He gradually surrendered the sense of omnipotence for a newfound sense of competence and mastery, with the associated emergence of vulnerability. His acceptance of his own vulnerability and limitations also led to his setting of limits on his own destructive behavior. He now looked to me for admiring mirroring while at the same time admiring and mirroring my efforts at tricks and exercises and expressing empathy when I failed.

During the treatment, I kept in close contact with Robert's school and was informed that he had begun to make an effort to learn and to ask for help. He could also accept limits and discipline from his teachers because he now perceived their efforts as help and not engulfment.

YVETTE

Yvette, a nine-year-old girl, was referred for fighting with peers and having temper tantrums in reaction to any change in her family or school situation. Yvette had already been to two therapists, and both treatments terminated after several weeks because Yvette sat sullenly and would not respond to the therapist's efforts to engage her in talk or play. The therapists and the mother had agreed that the child was not ready yet for treatment. Yvette's mother was herself a severely disturbed borderline patient currently in long-term treatment. The mother reported to her therapist that during Yvette's early childhood, the mother had experienced severe separation anxiety and would not allow Yvette out of her sight. Then she would feel trapped and imprisoned with the child and would experience murderous impulses toward her, which she fortunately did not act on.

Yvette's mother would become verbally abusive toward her whenever she misbehaved. She was overly involved in Yvette's everyday life and removed her from any activities, friendships, or classes if the child complained. Yvette, a Latino youngster, was referred by her mother's therapist.

Yvette insisted that she did not want to come for therapy. She initially sat silently and sullenly and would not look at me. I made no effort to engage her, and after a few minutes she rose and went out to her mother in the waiting room. She told her mother she did not like me, and the mother coaxed her to return. She sat silently for a time and then commented that I had an ugly beard. She drew pictures of my ugly beard and showed them to her mother. She continually went in and out of the therapy room during the first session. I never spoke afterward, and the mother asked if there was any point in returning. I told the mother she did fine and I would see her next week.

For the next three sessions, Yvette would sit silently and then draw pictures of my ugly beard to show to her mother. She then initiated a new activity by gathering all the chair and sofa pillows and cushions in the room and burying me where I sat beneath them. She piled them on me until I was completely buried and could not be seen, and then she brought her mother in to see. She buried and unburied me, laughing gleefully, while I remained as still as possible. Yvette's mother protested about her behavior, but I told her it was fine. Afterward, I explained to the mother that I wanted Yvette to bring all her behavioral problems into the session so I could see where she needed help.

During the next session, Yvette's mother told me that she had discovered Yvette drawing pictures of my ugly beard during the week between our sessions. On these pictures was a running commentary of "I hate Seinfeld. Seinfeld is ugly. Seinfeld's beard is ugly." She also drew a picture in which I breathed fire. I considered this activity as the first sign that she was developing a relationship with me and carrying around an internal image of me between sessions. She was relating to me by burying and unburying me— destroying and then re-creating me. Yvette was now in a full-blown ambivalent symbiosis. This phase reached its culmination one session when she brought in a bag of cookies. She played mommy. I played the child, and she fed me. She gave me the cookies, saying, "Aren't they good and yummy? Now eat all of them; they're good for you." After I ate a few, she said they were poisoned and would eat my insides out. She had me play at having a tummy ache. She then ordered me to play mommy and feed her the poison cookies. She had me play this role exactly as she had played it. First, I coaxed her to eat, saying that the cookies were good and yummy, and then after she ate a few, I told her that they were poisonous. She then rolled on the floor holding her aching tummy. She then called me a bad mommy for feeding her poisoned cookies.

Through this play interaction, Yvette recapitulated her early traumatic relationship with her mother. As noted earlier, Yvette's mother overprotected Yvette and would not let her out of her sight but then felt imprisoned and trapped by their closeness and had murderous impulses toward Yvette. The child reenacted the pathological symbiosis by having me offer good nurturance, which later proved to be poison.

I allowed Yvette to play out this ambivalent symbiotic sequence for as long as she needed to. After a time, she began to feed me good cookies and call me a "good child" and herself a "good mommy." She then had me play the good mommy feeding the good child good cookies. After we ate, she had us both lie on the floor and then said, "Good night mommy," and we played at sleeping. In this way, Yvette began to experience the therapeutic symbiosis in the transference.

In subsequent sessions, Yvette would sit in my chair and have me wheel her through the room. The sessions now shifted in tone from stormy and active to comforting and soothing. In the pictures she drew at home, I was no longer a man with the ugly beard breathing fire but rather a Christ-like figure caring for small animals and children.

IX

Interpreting the Tie
to the Bad Internal Object

Question: How does the therapist demonstrate to the patient the internal nature of the bad object?

Seinfeld: There are patients who enter treatment in an ambivalent symbiotic mode, which is acted out by the projection of the internal bad object onto the patient's everyday relationships. This type of patient experiences the therapist as a good external object serving as a "coach" to help the patient deal with the external person who is driving her crazy. In this way, the patient remains emotionally distant from the therapist in that the therapist does not become a significant, ambivalent, and symbiotic internal object. The following vignettes will illustrate how the therapist demonstrates the internal nature of the bad object.

MARILYN

Marilyn was a middle-aged woman who came to treatment stating her marriage of nearly thirty years was falling apart.

173

She reported having long-standing emotional problems, which her husband could no longer tolerate. She was clinging, demanding, and overly sensitive to criticism and rejection. Her husband protested that he needed distance and that if she did not stop taking her problems out on him, he would leave.

History

Marilyn's mother suffered a serious stroke when Marilyn was two years old and died when she was four years old. The patient grew up being taken care of by her father, grandmother, and other relatives. The father was a narcissistic, distant man who was more interested in finding a new wife to take care of him than in taking care of his daughter. The grandmother was the most loving and reliable caretaker, but she died when Marilyn was ten. The father remarried, and Marilyn at first idealized her glamorous stepmother. During Marilyn's adolescence, the stepmother became domineering, and physically abusive and pressured her to leave home. Marilyn met and married her husband after several months of courtship. At first, she felt he had saved her and that she did not need anyone as long as she had him. She described her early relationship to him as ideal and blissful but added that he was unemotional. He never expressed his feelings, though he did whatever she asked. Very early on, she became extremely jealous of his other relationships with family and friends. She lived in constant dread that he would abandon her. She often became enraged and accused him of not really loving her and then clung to him for reassurance, crying she could not live without him.

When her husband began to show resentment and distance himself, Marilyn went into a classical analysis for nine years. The analyst encouraged her to express all her fears, disappointments, and rage during the treatment sessions instead of with her husband. He pointed out the similarity between her husband's emotional shallowness and her father's selfishness and aloofness. He interpreted that her jealousy of her husband's relationships with family and friends referred back to her jealousy of her father's relationships with her mother and stepmother. He also interpreted that she clung to her husband because she feared independence and that her fear of being abandoned referred back to her early loss of her mother. She experienced these interpretations as intellectual and said they did not help her resolve her basic emotional insecurity and her dread of abandonment. Her treatment was terminated during a good period, when she and her husband were getting along. They agreed that she intellectually understood her problems but needed practice in putting her insights into action by becoming more independent.

When problems arose again between Marilyn and her husband, they tried marital therapy. They saw a therapist for a few months, and he concluded that Marilyn was too dependent and her husband too distant. He assigned them tasks in which she would behave more independently and he would try harder to relate. They managed those tasks for several weeks, but then Marilyn began to dread that her husband would inevitably leave. She felt herself falling into greater dread and at this point contacted me for treatment.

Question: In demonstrating to the patient the internal nature of the bad object, does the therapist ignore the behavior of the actual external object?

Seinfeld: The borderline patient's interpersonal relationships are complicated by the projective identification of the internal rejecting object situation into the external relationship. This view does not imply that the external other does not actually behave in a rejecting fashion. One might say that the borderline patient has a need for an external rejecting other, but I emphasize that this need serves the reinforcement and maintenance of the internal rejecting object. When a borderline patient obsesses about an external other, I consider this "other" as representing an internal object that the patient is bringing to treatment. On the one hand, the patient wants the therapist to "cure" the internal rejecting object. On the other hand, the patient places that object between himself and the therapist so that the internal bad object does not become activated in the ambivalent symbiotic transference.

In this situation, I first attempt to make the patient aware of how the external object represents an internal object and to demonstrate how she defensively and actively maintains her relationship to the bad internal object.

In the initial sessions, I asked Marilyn to tell me her story. I listened silently and gathered to myself the many examples of how she essentially viewed her husband sometimes as an all-good, providing, available mothering figure and at other times as an all-bad, depriving, rejecting mothering figure. Marilyn described how her husband had taken care of her at the beginning of their marriage and how his love protected her from feeling over-whelmed by the day-to-day living. I commented that his availability and care made her feel that all was right with herself and the world, just as the young child feels protected in the world when he experiences his mother as available, protective, and good. I said, "When you feel protected and cared for by him, you felt as if you were an accepted, worthy, and loved child and he was the accepting, comforting, and loving mother."

Marilyn described her terror and panic that her husband might leave her, noting that if he was in a bad mood or had a bad day at work, she felt certain that he was unhappy with her and that it would be only a matter of time before he left. I commented that her feelings of terror and panic were the same feelings that a young child would have if he feared that his mother might abandon him. I said that when this panic overwhelmed her, it was as if she was an unworthy, unwanted child and he was an abandoning, rejecting mother.

Question: How does the patient recognize that the internal object is not only a memory or image from the past but also an active, alive, present force in the patient's psyche?

Seinfeld: One of the most effective means to enable the patient to become aware of the current dynamic activity of the internal object is to explore his or her internal dialogues. I told Marilyn that I was interested not only with how she dealt with her husband in reality but also with how she dealt with him in her mind. I pointed out that we carry in our mind images of other people and ourselves and that we sometimes even carry on internal dialogues with the other, which can give rise to strong feelings. Marilyn replied that she often had imaginary fights with her husband, and I asked her to describe them.

She explained that she would accuse him of being overly involved with his sisters, mother, or some other person and that he was a fool for not recognizing how manipulative or selfish the other person was. She then imagined that he became angry, that he told her how crazy she was, and that he could not devote his every waking moment providing her with attention. If she did not leave him alone and give him space, he would leave. She became terrified and imagined begging him not to leave, and he took pity on her and reassured her. She initially felt relieved but then became angry that he did not love her but only pitied her. She would accuse him of not loving her, of putting everyone and everything before her, and he would become enraged and say he could not stand her any longer. The internal dialogue became an endless, vicious cycle and seemed as real as an actual quarrel.

Marilyn stated that her internal dialogues replicated her relationship to her husband. When running through such a dialogue, she would experience overwhelming terror, rage, relief, depression, anxiety, love, and hate. As she imagined her husband responding, it was as if his internal image took on a life of its own. She tended to have such fantasies when she was alone for a prolonged period, and I commented that on such occasions she did not feel alone because she kept herself company with her internal version of her husband.

When the patient is so dominated by the internal object, the therapist cannot arrive at anything like a realistic image of the other because what is being presented is an all-good or all-bad internal object that is colored or reinforced by the selected examples of all-good or all-bad behavior on the part of the external object. Each of Marilyn's pictures of her husband was supported by convincing evidence and examples. Such patients often present the "truth," but they describe the situation in a highly selective manner, such that the all-good or all-bad picture is presented and evidence to the contrary ignored. Therefore, in this initial phase of treatment, I emphasize the internal object situation. As patients gradually become aware that they are projectively identifying an internal object into the external object, they will begin to distinguish the two and present a more realistic picture of the external object.

I began to do this with Marilyn by repeating aloud her internal dialogue in a way that demonstrated the internal nature of the object. I said, "Let me see if I have this right. In your internal dialogue, you first express your anger and your jealousy at your husband. Then you have him or your image of him get angry at you and threaten to leave you. Next you are terrified and beg him not to leave, and then you have him pity you, and you then feel rejected that he pities you and doesn't love you, so you tell him so, and then you have him threaten to leave you."

Question: How do you get the patient to recognize that she is an active agent directing the internal rejecting object without blaming herself for this inner persecution?

Seinfeld: In reflecting on Marilyn's internal dialogue, I emphasized that it was her story, and she had the husband mistreat her. I immediately qualified I was not saying that she consciously or purposefully wanted her husband in reality to mistreat her or that she enjoyed or experienced masochistic pleasure in such mistreatment. I added, however, that she must be getting something out of this very unpleasant fantasy and that I wonder what it might be. She replied that the fantasy just replicates what actually occurs in the relationship. I assured her that I believed this was so, but then I wondered why she would repeatedly tell herself such an unpleasant daydream. It was her daydream, so she could do as she pleased with it. Sometimes, I said, when people have bad experiences, they daydream about a positive outcome. "I'm wondering why you maintain the bad outcome and make yourself feel the same bad way that your actual relationship with your husband makes you feel. Not only do you experience rejection by him in reality, but then you daydream about being rejected by him."

Marilyn then acknowledged that these fantasies of rejection severely depressed her. Sometimes she had these images in her mind before anything negative had occurred, and then her husband would take one look at her face, see trouble, and want to get away. She would then become enraged and accuse him of avoiding her, and the actual fight would begin.

I asked her to tell me more about this. Marilyn explained that every Sunday morning, she awakens and automatically thinks of everything her husband ever did wrong to her. She relived all these experiences as if they happened yesterday, even though many had occurred many years ago. She also thought of what he might do. She would get angry and imagine herself telling him off and then picture him rejecting her. She then became enraged as she was flooded by memories of every wrong he had ever committed. I commented that when the rejecting scenario had taken over in her mind, she was divorced from any positive experiences she may have had. By the time her husband would awaken, she would be in a rage. She would even be angry at him for sleeping when she had so much to say to him. I commented that his sleeping reinforced her rejecting image of him. She said to herself, "Why don't you wake up, you bastard?"

When he awakened, he saw the angry look on her face and tried to avoid her. Marilyn inevitably fell into this all-bad mental state every Sunday. This was the one day of the week that they could spend in a leisurely, enjoyable way, but it always ended in a terrible fight. I interpreted that she might activate the rejecting image of her husband in order to create distance between them. The fact that they had the opportunity to spend the day together and be close might give rise to her anger. I added that her husband played a part in this interaction as well, but it did seem that she activated this internal, rejecting scenario to create distance.

She said that my comments were diametrically opposed to what she had always been told about herself in previous therapies. She had always thought of herself as extremely dependent, as wanting closeness, and as clinging to her husband. Her previous therapists said that she sought the perfect union and then became enraged when she could not achieve it. She had never thought of herself as a person who wanted distance.

I did not yet interpret that her strong dependency needs give rise to merger anxiety and result in her creating distance through conjuring up her rage. Such interpretations should await the activation of the bad object situation in the transference. I commented that she does seek dependency as her therapists said but that she also seeks distance.

She reported gradual improvement in her relationship to her husband. As she experienced angry daydreams about her husband, she recalled my comments and thought the angry images were taking over. She caught herself searching for reasons to be angry. She now reported spending some relatively pleasant Sundays with her husband. For several sessions, she actively tried to distinguish when he was really behaving badly and when she was projecting the internal rejecting object onto him. As she sorted this out, she found that she could see herself in a more effective, less infinite fashion when he did create distance. She also began to understand his need for distance not as an abandonment of her as a worthless child but as the result of his own need to establish independence from his engulfing internal mother that he projected onto her. Thus, our sessions for a time consisted of our analysis of the internal object situation as projected into her husband. She and I made contact through the medium of her husband. He was our focus of discourse while at the same time his presence served as a barrier between us, preventing the activation of the bad object transference until she was ready. Therefore, the use of her husband as a transitional object served both contact and distance functions.

We explored the origin of the internal, rejecting object by attempting to recall when, during her childhood, she experienced a similar dread of abandonment and rejection. What came to her mind was the death of her mother. During the two years between her mother's stroke and death, when the patient was between the ages of two and four, she was in terror that her mother was ill and that something might happen to her. She recalled experiencing fear of rage on these occasions when she could not be with her bedridden mother. While discussing the threat and actual loss of her mother, Marilyn relived feelings of vulnerability, terror, rage, sadness, and abandonment. She recalled how the death of her mother left her in the hands of family members who she did not feel cared about her. She relived the feeling of vulnerability and recalled how she had to deny her terror because her family could not manage it.

Question: How does the therapist interpret the negative transference?

Seinfeld: As the patient becomes aware of the internal nature of the bad object, the patient begins to transfer the bad object situation from everyday interpersonal relationships into the transference. I repeatedly and directly interpret the internal bad object situation and its activation in the transference.

For Marilyn, the need for the good mother and vulnerable self emerged directly in the ambivalent symbiotic transference. Once Marilyn recalled how she had to deny her vulnerability after her mother died, she came into our session complaining of the long trip to my office. For the first time, I saw the angry facial expression she had described. She complained that she might have an accident driving in crazy Manhattan traffic. She feared she would be mugged, her car could be broken into, and the air pollution aggravated her allergies. She said my office was stuffy and closed in and asked whether I somehow could find another office.

She reported that after leaving my office, she had felt terrified and vulnerable, just as she had as a child after her mother died. The world seemed frightening and dangerous. I had opened a Pandora's box. She was driving her family crazy. She was taking all her frustration out on her family and husband. She felt they did not care about her. She criticized them and felt they could not do anything right, yet she feared they would abandon her. She felt she needed me more than before, but I was far away, and this thought made her not want to come.

I interpreted that she had distanced herself from me emotionally, so I seemed far away physically. I acknowledged that it was a long trip from her home to my office, but when she felt better about our relationship in her mind, she enjoyed the trip as a pleasant day in the city. Now that she felt bad about our relationship, the trip and the city felt bad and overwhelming.

She acknowledged the connections I was making and then discussed how bad her early family life was and how they were all stuck with one another. In our last session, she had realized how enraged she had been with her family after her mother's death. She immediately had to deny her anger at them because "you can't bite the hand that feeds you." Following her mother's death, she was abruptly moved from a crib to a large bed in which she had felt lost, and she had to start walking to and from school by herself every day. She felt extremely vulnerable; she was so small, and the world seemed so dangerous. She had to swallow her fear and her rage and enact the part of her family's view of a "good girl."

I said that as a little girl she had to swallow her rage about the death of her mother and her uncaring family and that the rage had to go somewhere, so she saw and felt it in the surrounding world, into which she was suddenly thrown and which seemed so menacing. I said that this weak fear that her current family would abandon her and did not care about her was a reliving of her feelings in her family of her early childhood. I said that because I was understanding the impact of the loss of her mother and her early vulnerability, she was experiencing greater dependency on me as a potential good mothering supportive figure. All week, she felt I was very far away, that she would never get to me, just as during childhood she had wanted her mother but could not be reunited with her. She experienced me as abandoning her and was dissatisfied with the family she was remaining with. I said she was placing me far away in her mind because her dependency on me frightened her but then she felt abandoned by me. In this session, Marilyn became calmer as I repeatedly interpreted the activation of the bad object transference.

MYRNA

Myrna is a forty-year-old single mother of an adolescent daughter. The husband left the family several years ago and remains out of contact. The seventeen-year-old daughter, Peggy, is living away from home at a private school.

Myrna has been a public school teacher for fifteen years and is respected and valued by her colleagues. She lives by herself in a tastefully furnished apartment. Although on the surface of things she seems to do well, she says that no one could imagine how much she suffers.

In treatment, she initially related to me in the same appropriate fashion she described in relating to others. She has been seeing a man for eight years and is dissatisfied but cannot leave him. While dating her all these years, this man, Joe, complains he still has not met the right woman. Every Saturday night, Joe dates another woman. Myrna says she wishes to see Joe on Saturday nights, but he complains that she is too demanding of his time and attention, that she is not the right woman for him and that he has no intention of changing.

Myrna says that this relationship is crazy, masochistic, and limited. She gives further examples. He takes her to a restaurant and complains the food she orders is too expensive. She says she will pay for herself so that she can order whatever she likes. He becomes resentful when she pays. Either way, she cannot enjoy her dinner.

Question: How does the therapist explore what keeps the patient involved in a poor relationship? Is the patient hoping the other will change? Is the patient merely masochistic?

Seinfeld: The therapist inquired, "Well, if what you describe is so, why don't you leave him? What is in it for you?"

She said, "The times when we are close it is good. His body smells so good. He is into his body. It's nearly an obsession. He lifts weights daily. He's fastidious about his appearance. He always wears cologne and smells of fresh soap. I become jealous. He cares more for his body than he cares for me. Narcissus. I don't really care for sex. He's not a great lover. He's really only interested in himself. But I like closeness and holding. There's still no reason to stay with him. Whatever is good does not outweigh the suffering."

The major reasons Myrna presents for not leaving Joe are her fear of suffering and the hope that he will change. She says, "If I leave him, I'm afraid I'll have no one. I'm afraid to be all alone. Several times, when I was angry at him for seeing other women, I went out with other men. Even if they treated me as if I were special and acted as if they cared about me, I always returned to Joe. If someone treats me well, I start to find flaws in them. With Joe, I become addicted to the highs and lows."

"Tell me about the highs and lows," I said.

"I always feel like Joe is dangling a carrot in front of me," she replied. "He won't call, and I won't see him for awhile. Then I'll

185

get angry and be about to give up. Then he puts out feelers— some show of interest. I get all excited. I feel as if he cares for me finally. But as soon as I bite, he's no longer interested. I'm high for a while hoping that he cares, but then I go down into the emotional dumps. Sometimes I believe he is sadistic and plays with me. He wants me in his life but not too much."

The first several months of treatment are comprised of "Joe" sessions. Myrna describes in detail the ups and downs with Joe. On occasion, her daughter or female friends enter the picture. During these occasions, they are described in "Joe" terms. Her daughter does not telephone as promised or would rather spend the weekend with friends. She gives so much to Peggy, but her daughter is unappreciative, uncaring, or she tries to get together with friends when Joe is not around but they are unavailable. Myrna is enraged that her brother does not invite her for dinner, that her daughter does not visit, and that her friends have other plans.

Listening to Myrna over the months, I get the sense that the other—which includes predominantly Joe but also sometimes her daughter, brother, and friends—accused her of being smothering, demanding, and entitled and is experienced by her as rejecting, distancing, and uncaring.

"Peggy has no sense of money," Myrna says. "She buys clothes with whatever she earns from her part-time job. I never did that. I saved all the money I earned when I was her age. This weekend she's going to the beach with friends. She could be working. I don't understand her job. Her boss gives her off whenever she wishes. Instead of saving her money for school, she spends it all with her friends. The kids at her school are wealthy. I believe they are a bad influence on her. All she thinks about is her friends, herself, and having a good time."

The weekend Myrna refers to will be one without Joe. He is going hunting. She wants Peggy to return from school to keep her company, but she does not come out and say this. Instead, she complains of Peggy's self-preoccupation, irresponsibility, and choice of friends. She had tried to say as much to Peggy, but the latter accused her of being too demanding. Peggy, who knows about the Joe agenda, retorted, "What's the matter? Joe isn't around this weekend? You want me home to cry on my shoulder. You always want me to take care of you. I'm not doing it."

Question: How does the therapist demonstrate that the common characteristics of these disappointing people in the patient's life are the manifestations of an internal bad object?

Seinfeld: A certain motif can be identified in Myrna's mode of relating to the other, comprising Joe, Peggy, her brother, and her friends.

Myrna complains that the "other" puts itself and others before her. Joe puts his body and girlfriends before her. Her brother puts his Sunday newspaper and his wife and children before her. Her neighbors and friends put relaxing and watching television before her. Myrna does not present these complaints directly but instead criticizes the other's way of life. Furthermore, she relates in such a way as to provoke others into calling her demanding, entitled, and smothering, and they in turn make themselves increasingly unavailable. Myrna is therefore dominated psychically by an internal bad object situation in which she views the internal bad object as rejecting and self-preoccupied and she becomes demanding, entitled, and smothering toward it. However, if Myrna loses hope in connecting, it excites her only enough to keep her involved.

When I first intervene with such patients, I focus almost exclusively on the internal object situation. This is especially true if their behavior is not seriously self-destructive. Therefore, I remain neutral about what they do with the external relationship and address most of my remarks to the internal object relationship. In a sense, I do not take the external relationship so seriously. By this attitude, I convey to the patient that the external object is not fully real but rather is a reflection of the internal object.

When Myrna asked me fairly soon if she should leave Joe, I shrugged and told her she could leave or stay. When she was disturbed about something she said or did with Joe, I would say, "So?" Before long, she would say, "I know that you think what I actually do with Joe or what he thinks of me doesn't matter much. You think all of this is really about something else?"

Question: How does the therapist get to the something else and illustrate what the something else is?

Seinfeld: I initially set up a preliminary framework to address the internal object situation. First, I made Myrna aware that the common complaint about the "other" was that the other put everyone and everything before her. When she told me of her complaints about Joe, I asked what she gets out of the relationship. She told me how she loved the cuddling and holding. She does not really enjoy the sex, but it is something she gives up so that she will not be abandoned. I therefore discussed with her how she seeks a certain nurturing or mothering in that cuddling and holding; being taken care of and fearing abandonment are feelings that a child experiences in a parent-child relationship. This makes sense to her and leads to a discussion about her relationship with her mother.

Her mother was a very narcissistic woman. She was beautiful and glamorous, interested only in her appearance and in seeking attention from men. Myrna suffered more from neglect than from active abuse. When she brought home an excellent report card, her mother would respond, "That's nice," as if her mind was a million miles away. She did not feel her mother was so much threatened as she was indifferent to Myrna's achievements.

She helped her mother by praising her appearance and doing household chores. Years later, she asked her mother why she did not seem more attentive or concerned about her school performance or outside achievements, and the mother said, "I never had to worry about you. You always were excellent."

Myrna adds that her mother was not all bad. After Myrna had helped her in some way, her mother would allow her to cuddle with her, and she would smell her mother's scented skin or brush her lovely hair. Myrna's mother had a very likeable, appealing personality, and when Myrna grew older, she loved talking to her. Many of her friends envied her relationship with her mother because she was more like an older sister or friend than a mother.

The one thing she recalled being angry at her mother for was that her mother was much more interested in Myrna's brother and that her mother was much more interested in going out with men and leaving Myrna and her brother home alone. Although she sometimes felt jealous of her brother, she also experienced him as actively supportive, especially in adult life, in that he would often invite her to his home on vacations and holidays.

During our sessions, as she told me of her anger at Joe for his self-absorption, I would remind her of her mother's self-absorption. My comments reminded her of how her mother paid so much attention to her own body and to grooming while ignoring Myrna. She connected her other's preoccupation with her body to Joe's preoccupation with his. I remarked on how she felt jealous of her mother's preoccupation with herself, but she repressed that jealousy; it was now emerging in her anger at Joe for his self-love.

When she would come in and complain that Joe was leaving her alone on Saturday nights to go out with other women, I reminded her of how her mother left her alone to go out with other men. I interpreted how she remains attached to a mother who puts herself and her lovers before Myrna.

I emphasized that the issue is not simply that Joe reminds her of her mother from the past but that she remains attached currently to this mother in her mind and that this attachment is displaced onto Joe.

Myrna asked whether she allows Joe to mistreat her because it resembles how her mother mistreated her. I focused on how she always thinks of Joe as rejecting her by placing others before her and on how she obsesses about this image even when he is not present, and I emphasized that this image really refers to her mother. The actual Joe reinforced the rejecting image of the mother. Whenever she broached the subject of Joe, I would talk to her about her mother. When she said, "I'm upset that Joe did not call," I said, "You're thinking of yourself as not cared for by your mother."

Sometimes she would plead, "Do you think he cares for me?"

I would reply, "Who knows? What is the difference? He's just Joe. You are wondering if your mother cares for you."

Sometimes she was upset that she was not more assertive. Joe disappointed her. Instead of expressing her anger, she would plead and cry. She now felt that she was weak and feared he would see her as such. I said that in her early relationship to her mother, she did not protest or cry when frustrated because she feared her mother would be completely fed up and abandon her. I reminded her that we were speaking only of "Mother Joe."

When she brought up her fear of being abandoned by Joe, I would say, "So what if he leaves? What difference does it make in your life? You describe your relationship with him as predominantly painful. You are only terrified because it is your mother leaving you as a helpless infant. You continue to live those early terrors in your mind."

She replied, "All I do is suffer over him anyway. How often do I mention something positive? In reality, I do not lose much if he leaves. I lose this pain. I'd probably be better off."

At this point, as she recognized that the relationship with Joe was more bad than good, the therapist actively supported her inclination to end the relationship and face the underlying terror. Joe and Myrna eventually agreed that it would be better to end their relationship, that they were not going anywhere and just gave each other grief.

Myrna became quite distressed about being alone. It became quite apparent that she was psychically dominated by a bad internal object situation, and it became easier to address this situation through direct interpretations. As Joe gradually faded in her thoughts, Myrna became upset about her daughter and brother. Since she was no longer seeing Joe, she expected her brother to invite her to his house and her daughter to always call. On one particular weekend when her brother and daughter were unavailable, Myrna complained of being all alone, that no one cares if she lived or died, that she might as well commit suicide.

"I don't quite see things that way," I said.

"Well, how do you see them?" she asked.

"All that you're talking about is spending a weekend alone. Solitary confinement can drive a person crazy. If you were locked in a room by yourself without human contact, yes, you would eventually go psycho. You are reacting to spending a couple of days alone as if you were in solitary confinement. Do you see that what is making it so bad is what is going on in your mind, that you are experiencing yourself as abandoned and unwanted?"

191

The internal bad object situation is shifting from Joe to her daughter, her brother, and her friends. Myrna associated being alone with being abandoned.

Question: In this instance, the therapist challenged and interpreted Myrna's sense of being rejected. Isn't it possible that Myrna will experience the therapist as unempathic for ignoring Myrna's subjective sense that the brother and daughter reject her?

Seinfeld: If the therapist is too quick to empathize with Myrna's loneliness, this will intensify her belief that she is being victimized and support the projection of the bad object. At the same time, the therapist cannot ignore Myrna's feelings that the brother and daughter are not as supportive as she wished. The therapist handled this dilemma by saying, "You are thinking of yourself as unwanted and your brother and daughter as putting you last. You are carrying an image of yourself as rejected and as others rejecting you, only the actors keep changing. Instead of Joe, it is your brother and daughter. Now I'm not saying that they are not selfish. They might be as bad or even worse than you say. We can say for certain that you are not getting as much support as you wished. But the consequence is that you have to spend two days on your own. I think what troubles you is not that you have to spend a day alone but that you feel abandoned by your mother again. It is possible that if the people in your life were more supportive, the abandoned feeling would not be so intense."

She replied, "Let me see if I have it right. You're saying it's not really what they are doing to me. That doesn't mean that they're right. But it's really what I'm doing to myself. I see that. I'm acting like I'm being tortured the way I'm carrying on. It's actually quite comfortable here. I have my stereo, my books. There's a lot of reading I'd like to do. I can even go out. Then I go back to work.

I'm doing this to myself. Joe, my brother, my daughter. It is all the same. They're all my mother. Mother's Day again. My brother hasn't been entirely bad. He said I could come next weekend. He acted concerned. I kept telling him I have no family, that he doesn't care. I pushed him away. He became angry and said he doesn't care, and I hung up."

X

Interpreting Splitting
of the Transference

Question: How does the therapist address the transference when the patient splits off the negative aspect onto people in the external world while idealizing the therapist?

Seinfeld: In the previous chapter, we described patients who enter treatment already involved in a symbiotic relationship with an external object. In the scenario you question, the patient initially idealizes the therapist and splits off the negative component onto persons in the external reality. They experience the external objects in their lives as exciting but nongratifying, persecuting, or enmeshing. The bad object transference often becomes apparent as the patient eventually becomes angry or disappointed in the therapist for not protecting him or her from the bad persecutory objects. I will demonstrate how these issues become manifest through clinical vignettes.

LORRAINE

The patient, a single woman in her mid-thirties, was seen by a female therapist for a year. The therapist believed the case to be relatively easy to handle. The patient maintained her own business and apartment. She described herself as an independent type but said she was sometimes prone to take care of others at her own expense. She described two relationships as the nemesis of her life. The first was with her mother, an alcoholic, who lived alone and often called on the patient for help. Lorraine, the oldest of three siblings, always responded when her mother needed her. Her father had left the family when Lorraine was three years old. She grew up missing him and hoped that he would return or the mother would remarry. The mother claimed that the father's desertion had driven her to drink, but Lorraine sometimes wondered if the mother's drinking might have driven the father to leave. The mother had depended on the patient to raise her younger siblings. She conscientiously cared for her siblings and served as a confidante for her mother. In turn, the mother told the patient that she was the best child in the world and that she could never get along without her.

In her late adolescence, the patient met Felix, whom she described as the second nemesis of her life. She immediately fell in love with this handsome, personable, adventurous man. He told her that he desperately needed her to straighten out his life. He was unemployed and used drugs. For the first time, her mother was unable to control her. Her mother pleaded with her not to turn off with him. Lorraine believed her mother to be right, but she could not control her feelings. Felix found a job, swore off drugs, and said he was ready to start a new life with Lorraine. They married. Felix quit his job and went back to drugs, and Lorraine supported him and his drug abuse. She felt fed up and believed Felix married her to be taken care of and not because he loved her. After many fights and threats on his part to leave, she finally told him to go and never return.

The patient eventually started her own business and learned she could live without Felix. Nevertheless, Felix and her mother continued to plague her. Her mother asked her to visit when she had some scheme in mind. She would want something from one of her children, and the patient was selected to persuade her sibling to do whatever the mother had in mind. Lorraine felt exploited and controlled but could not tolerate her mother's anger or disapproval. She also felt a sense of well-being and security when the mother said, "You are the only one I can depend upon. What would I do without you?"

The patient had not entirely rid herself of Felix. He would often come around in trouble, and she would bail him out. Sometimes he needed a place to sleep. She did not allow him to return permanently, but she remained available.

In the course of her treatment, it became apparent that Lorraine was still very much emotionally involved with Felix and her mother. She would report that she spent much of her time ruminating over how vulnerable she was and thinking that her mother and Felix were interested only in what they could get from her. She became aware that she felt comforted when they spoke of needing her because this meant that they would not abandon her. She felt that her only choices were to be a good, special, dependable, savior child or to be the unwanted, unloved child abandoned for her worthlessness. These choices resulted in two split-off sets of internalized object relations: the good child defending against the unwanted, unloved, worthless child.

Question: How does the therapist help bridge these split-off sets of object relations units?

Seinfeld: When the patient first presents herself as a perfectly loving, giving, and caring individual, the therapist should not immediately challenge this grandiose identity. It must be remembered that the patient's image of herself as all-giving is her only source of self-esteem. She felt good about herself only when she helped someone else. In accepting Lorraine's goodness for being helpful, the therapist became, in the transference, the mother who valued her for these traits. The patient boasted about all that she did for her mother, for Felix, and for friends in need. She repeatedly expressed the value that "it is good to go out of your way for others," and the therapist nodded and accepted her comments. Underlying this comment was the unspoken communication that no one goes out of his way for her. As she told of incidents in which she helped others, she began to express resentment. As her complaints grew, the therapist introduced the idea that "it is good for you to help others, and it is good that you care, but when it is at your expense, it gets you in trouble."

Lorraine told how her mother and Felix took advantage of her, explaining that both talked of how good it was to be helpful but that they always seemed to be on the helped instead of the helping side of the equation. The therapist now commented on some of the similarities between the alcoholic mother and the drug-addicted Felix. The patient began to recognize that they both represented an object that she feared would abandon her if she did not help it.

Lorraine was able to make good use of the therapy. She would think about the therapist's remarks between sessions and draw on a comforting image of the therapist when she feared that the bad object might abandon her. She told the therapist that she was the only person who ever helped her selflessly. She and the therapist were alike in that they both helped others and wanted nothing in return, whereas her mother and Felix were hypocrites who spoke of help only so that they could be on the receiving end.

The issue of the bad object transference emerged after the therapist told Lorraine about her impending vacation. The patient responded by talking about her frustration and resentment of Felix and about her mother. The therapist noted that they were not actually treating Lorraine any worse than usual. The therapist said that Lorraine might be directing her anger about the therapist's vacation onto Felix and her mother. The patient disagreed. She insisted that she was not angry at the therapist's vacation, that this would be irrational. Everyone takes a vacation, including the patient, and anyway she was not angry at the therapist.

Before the vacation, Lorraine complained about Felix and her mother. She began to wonder whether therapy was helping. She had felt better for a time over the past year, but how could this have lasted when Felix and her mother were such rats? The therapist could not change them. What she needed was to meet new people, good people. She needed to meet a man. How could the therapist help her meet a good man? She had not wanted to say anything, but she has been thinking about this for a while. She needed to meet men, and the therapy was not helping her do that. Laughing, she said she was not blaming the therapist. After all, she did not expect the therapist to introduce her to men. But maybe she should stop coming because her real problem is that she needs a man, and the therapist could not help her with that.

The last comment about how the therapist cannot help her meet a man is the mark of the underlying bad object transference. Lorraine's predominant mode of relatedness to her mother on the conscious level in her childhood was that both she and her mother valued helpfulness and caring. On occasion, she also thought of her mother as bad for having deprived her of a father. Maybe the mother had even deliberately driven the father out so that Lorraine would have only the mother to relate to. The child must therefore be close to the mother and serve the mother's needs, and no man could ever come between them. If the child does not serve the mother's needs, then she would no longer be the special savior child but rather would become an unworthy, unloved child that the mother would abandon.

The patient has thus far expressed to the mother therapist that she is the savior child. The therapist, like the mother, accepts and values her as the savior child. The therapist then helps the patient not sacrifice herself entirely to save Felix and her natural mother. This is how the therapist begins to serve as a bridge between the patient's good and bad object relations units. The patient consciously says, "We are just alike; we are the only ones who value selfless help. Mother and Felix are hypocrites." However, the patient may unconsciously understand the therapist's interpretations to mean "stop devoting yourself to your mother and Felix and devote yourself *exclusively* to me: thou shall place no other mothers before me."

Question: When the patient states that the therapist wants her to be devoted exclusively to her, is she reliving the loss of her father?

Seinfeld: Felix and the actual mother represent the father whom the mother therapist is getting rid of. Lorraine complains that the therapist has taken away her bad objects but does not provide her with a new father. The patient says, "I can see now that Felix and my mother exploit me. I no longer want to help them at my own expense. I can see that they give me nothing in return. I'm disgusted with them now. But how can this therapy help? You cannot introduce me to new people or help me find a man." The issue of finding a man, which seems to come out of nowhere, is actually an association to the loss of the mother and Felix. Lorraine is reliving in the transference the early cry to the mother, "Bring back my father!" The patient complains that the therapist cannot help. Her statement referring to the therapist's ineffectiveness is a cover-up for the unconscious belief that the bad mother is depriving her of the father because the mother wants to get rid of the father as a buffer between them. She threatens to leave therapy because she perceives the bad mother as threatening her with merger and with abandonment if she refuses to merge. The impending vacation, a symbolic threat of abandonment, triggers the bad object transference.

Question: Should the therapist not have helped Lorraine separate from Felix and her mother since this resulted in her feeling threatened with merger?

Seinfeld: The interpretations and comments about the role played by Felix and the mother in the patient's psyche were accurate and led to a reliving of the bad mother transference in a disguised form. This development is necessary, though the therapist needs to interpret that the patient is threatened by both merger and abandonment and perceives the therapist as a bad mother getting rid of the father (Felix and the actual mother). It is not enough to simply interpret the patient's anger at Felix and her mother as a displacement of anger at the therapist.

The next case illustrates similar dynamics with a much more disturbed patient. Afterward, the two cases will be compared.

201

WANDA

Wanda is a rather wealthy, married individual. The therapist, who has seen the patient for only three months, believes the patient is deteriorating. For the first few sessions, the patient manifested a rather unrealistic idealization in the transference. She described her current life situation, and the therapist simply listened. Wanda enthusiastically said, "I love coming here. You understand everything. I feel I can talk to you about anything. Could I come more frequently?" At times the patient remarked on the therapist's clothing. She would say, "Oh, you dress just like me. We have the same taste. That skirt must have been very expensive."

After the first few sessions, Wanda embarked on a crash liquid diet. She attributed her efforts to diet to the treatment even though the therapist had not offered encouragement and had taken an exploratory stance. The patient, who was not considerably overweight, seemed manic about the diet.

In subsequent sessions, Wanda became distraught about her life situation. She complained that her husband did not earn enough, that she had married a failure. She devalued the flowers he gave her, saying that he was cheap and should have bought jewelry. She saw the other people and situations in her life as all bad.

The therapist was confused. Only a month before, she had described her life in glowing, enthusiastic terms. She had the most wonderful husband in the world, a man who made a terrific living, who regularly bought her flowers. She loved her life and her work. Now her job was "worthy of a mental midget," and she hated every last one of her coworkers. How could therapy help? The therapist could not change her job, her husband, or her life. She was sick of talking. What good did it do? She was fed up. Maybe she should stop coming.

In listening to the patient describe her terrible life, the therapist had completely forgotten about the diet, and the patient had not mentioned it. Then something Wanda said about food reminded the therapist. She learned that the patient was still on her diet. Many of the activities that enabled the patient to maintain her manic defense related to social activities that centered around food. In the past few weeks, she had had to curtail those activities because of the diet. The diet had been the precipitant to much of her current state of deprivation.

The therapist missed the rapidly growing bad object transference that had resulted in the patient's acting-out behavior. In a sense, Wanda was correct in attributing the diet to the "benefits" of therapy. Because of the regressed, primitive level of her dependency needs, she perceived the therapist's understanding and acceptance as intensely exciting. She reacted to the therapist as an exciting breast she could not get enough of. For example, she immediately wanted to see the therapist more frequently and reacted with manic enthusiasm to the therapist's understanding acceptance.

M. Klein (1959) has noted that intense oral dependency in the transference can give rise to envy and hatred of the breast that contains everything on the earth that one needs. I am translating Klein's view to refer not only to oral instinctual need but also to the need for empathy and emotional care. The therapist's empathy and acceptance give rise to the patient's excited dependency and envy on a very primitive level. The clinical evidence of envy can first be seen in the patient's remark about the therapist's clothing and how she and the therapist dress alike. Immediately following this remark, the patient began her crash diet and then complained that no one in her life gave her enough. The diet unconsciously referred to the therapist as an exciting object. Wanda was not going to take in any more of the therapist's empathic breast because it was exciting too much dependency and envy. Her refusal of solid food referred to an unconscious equation of solid food, breast, and empathy. She then immediately complained that no one in her life gave her anything good. These complaints referred to her state of empathic starvation: She was no longer taking in the therapist's empathy. Her complaints were also triggered by her envy of the therapist. If others would only give her more, then she would not need to envy and depend on the therapist. In turn, she could devalue the therapist and her help by saying, in effect, "How can your empathy help me when I'm so deprived of the material things in life?" In essence, her insatiable need for nonhuman exciting objects was a mental construction serving her as a defense against her need for human empathy.

The therapist could have immediately and directly interpreted the crash diet as a reaction to her excited need for the therapist. The therapist could have also empathized with her need to maintain her autonomy and not totally surrender to excited dependency. In addition, the therapist may have interpreted her sense of deprivation with everyone in her life as self-induced starvation from the therapist's empathy and also as envy in feeling that the therapist has everything and she has nothing.

Question: Why is it that the first patient, Lorraine, maintained a good object transference for nearly a year, a much longer time than the second patient, Wanda? Is the distinction in the nature of their internalized object relations units?

Seinfeld: Lorraine possesses a stronger positive self and object representation unit, which protects her from the internal bad object situation.

An important clinical distinction is the way in which the bad object transference emerges in the two cases. In the case of Lorraine, the therapist does something in reality that is bad from the patient's perspective: She goes away on vacation. In the case of Wanda, the bad object transference is activated spontaneously, not from a real event, such as a planned vacation, but rather from the threat of the relationship itself. The therapist as a hoped-for good object stimulated the patient's insatiable object need and oral envy. She defended against deprivation by going on a diet, which created a psychic state of oral dependence, enabling her to split off the exciting transference object onto the external objects in her life. In starving herself, she created a situation in which she felt deprived and irritable with everyone except the therapist.

Lorraine is protected from the bad object situation by a narcissistic positive self and object representation, which she constitutes as a good savior child admired by her depressed mother for her helping qualities. With some other patients, the narcissistic positive self and object representation unit consists of a special child with special gifts receiving unconditional praise from an admiring object. These positive self and object representation units are pathological in the sense of being split off from the other sector of the personality and serving to defend against the emergence of the other aggressively cathected self and object representation unit. This also has adaptive aspects for the patient. For instance, Lorraine is able to take care of others even if at her own expense and is not totally at the mercy of the bad object situation. The patient's positive self and object unit is readily reinforced by the therapist's empathic mirroring of the grandiose self. With such narcissistic patients, the therapist has the dual task of initially enforcing the positive self and object representation unit through empathy and later interpreting the split-off defensive aspect so that it can be integrated into the personality.

Wanda, who is a severe borderline personality, does not possess a consolidation pathological grandiose self that consistently protects her from the bad object situation through a prolonged narcissistic transference. Instead, the activation of the mirroring transference is precipitously and spontaneously aborted by the bad object situation. With the severe borderline patient, the therapist must actually build the positive self and object representations while interpreting the massive, acute bad object transference activations.

HELEN

This patient, a woman in her twenties, worked as a commercial artist and lived with a female roommate. She was separated from her husband and was planning on divorce. She was being seen by a male therapist whom I supervised.

Helen began treatment after separating from her husband and reported to the therapist that the separation was the result of her husband's alcohol and drug abuse. They had been married for several years, and throughout this time she had tried to persuade her husband to go to Alcoholics Anonymous, a drug program, or marital therapy, but he refused. After a while, Helen saw no hope for him changing and decided that she must leave him. She told the therapist her story and was pleased that he believed her and supported her decision.

She stated, "My mother and my brother say that I exaggerate my husband's problems and that I should accept him as he is. My father tried to sexually abuse me when I was a teenager, and when I told my mother, she didn't believe me and accused me of making up stories." The therapist empathizes with her experience of her mother as not taking her seriously. The patient replied, "You are the first person ever to take me seriously. I like you a lot. I wish I could meet a man like you."

Over the course of a year's treatment, the patient would come into sessions complaining that the men in her life did not respect her and either subtly or overtly viewed her as an inferior female or that her mother or brother did not take her seriously or that her colleagues or roommate tried to take advantage of her. The therapist empathized with her perceptions and helped her assert herself and not permit others to manipulate her. She, in turn, would praise the therapist as the only person in her life who ever understood her.

Gradually, minor problems arose that troubled the therapist. The patient would, on occasion, say she had nothing to say. She became visibly uncomfortable and asked whether she still needed to come. The therapist wondered whether her positive feelings for him made her uncomfortable. The patient would talk for a time about how different he was, and she would verbalize affectionate and sexual feelings toward him. The therapist became uncomfortable that she viewed everyone in her life as all bad and as injuring her. Yet she presented a good case that many of these people did, in fact, treat her badly. The therapist raised the issue of whether she was not in some way drawn to people who treat her badly. She readily acknowledged that she appeared to be drawn to people similar to her father. Her father abused alcohol, disrespected and exploited women, and was highly narcissistic. She seemed to be drawn to similar men even though she quickly became disappointed in them. But these insights made little difference in her relatedness in the treatment sessions. She often had nothing to say and thought about dropping out.

When the therapist first presented this to me, I wondered whether the patient's stated view that the therapist was different from anyone in her life was the entire story. Could it be that the bad object aspect of the transference was being split off into those in her environment and thereby reinforcing her view of them as all bad? I suggested that the therapist should not immediately interpret this to the patient but that he should keep it in mind when he saw her.

The therapist planned to take a short vacation. In the beginning of the next session, he explored the patient's feelings about this. She felt a little angry but considered her anger to be unreasonable; after all, she had a right to take a vacation, and he was not doing so to personally reject her. She then changed the subject to the bus ride on the way to the session.

"This guy got on the bus. He and his friend sat directly across from me. I couldn't believe what he was saying. In the loudest voice he was saying the most terrible things about women. He was discussing all the things he had done to some woman and teaching his friend how to treat a woman to get what you want. He said all this with no regard for who heard him. In fact, he looked directly at me to see my response. I gave him a dirty look. I can't believe how people are."

The therapist empathized with her feelings. She then discussed how her father, her brother, and the men she dates have similar views about women.

The fact that she discussed the man on the bus immediately after the discussion around the therapist's vacation might suggest some association between the therapist and the man on the bus. I asked the therapist what the patient had said the man on the bus did to this woman in the scene that he had depicted to his friend. He said that the patient had not volunteered the specifics and that he did not inquire. I wondered why. The therapist said the thought had occurred to him, but he had felt "funny" asking what the man on the bus had described doing to this unknown woman. I asked what he had felt funny about, and he said that he had imagined that the patient might wonder about his motives for wanting to know the specifics. She might feel offended that he would ask and that he would expect her to repeat what might have been a very vulgar description of the treatment of a woman. I then suggested that he might be inhibited in this way in defending against her viewing him as a bad object.

In the next session, as the patient continued to discuss the men in her life, he asked what the common characteristic was that such men felt about women. She said that women are dispensable to them. He then asked whether she felt that way about him—that women, she in particular, were dispensable to him in that he was now planning to leave her for a time to go on vacation. She agreed that the word *dispensable* was apt for how she felt. She said his going away made her feel disposed of, but at the same time she did not feel she could reasonably protest. He wondered if she did not use her reasonableness to protect their relationship. She said she feared becoming unreasonable toward him. She feared that if she became demanding, dependent, or angry, he would find her a headache and get pissed off as all the other persons in her life did. She said she was more reasonable with him than with other persons in her life. She felt that she must act like a grown-up. When she became angry or had unreasonable expectations, she reminded herself that theirs was a professional relationship and that she should behave in a mature manner. She could not tolerate it if she became demanding or angry and he rejected her as everyone else in her life did.

Question: But it sounds as if she is trying to be cooperative about focusing in the therapeutic work. Isn't this the therapeutic alliance?

Seinfeld: This case illustrates how the therapeutic alliance in such cases can sometimes be a resistance to the activation of the bad object transference. The patient subsequently revealed that in the silent, uncomfortable sessions in which she had nothing to say to the therapist and thought of leaving treatment, she had fleeting negative thoughts about him. She would sometimes say to herself, "I don't really know anything about him. I don't really know how he feels abut women, how he treats women in his personal life, what his political beliefs are. Yes, he says the right thing here, but he's trained and paid to do so. This is how he is professionally. But who knows what he is really like?"

Her questions about what the therapist might really be like referred to her view of him as a bad object. She revealed that she believed that if she expressed what she was really like, then the personal instead of the professional him would react. She imagined that the personal him might be impatient, intolerant, and rejecting. She later explained that when she was a child, if she made demands on her father or expressed anger, he would become impatient, rejecting, and intolerant. She attributed these characteristics to the personal side of the therapist and behaved so this bad side of him would not emerge in their interaction.

This patient had therefore two relationships to the therapist. On the surface, she was a good, understanding, cooperative patient relating to an empathic, caring, sensitive therapist. This idealizing transference was neither a mere illusion nor solely a defense but in fact reflected one side of reality. To this patient who was sexually abused by her father and mistreated by nearly all others throughout her life, the therapist's professional stance and empathy provided an important experience of being understood, valued, and considered worthwhile. At the same time, on another level, she related to the therapist as the bad, exciting, sadistic, rejecting father/object.

As Fairbairn states, the therapist must be a good enough object in reality for the patient to release the bad internal object in the transference. The uncomfortable sessions when the patient had nothing to say were an indication that it was time to interpret the defensive aspect of the idealizing transference and the split bad object situation.

Question: The clinical cases you have described for the most part demonstrate the bad object transference in pre-oedipal conditions. Does the bad object transference ever manifest itself in oedipal clinical material and, if so, how?

Seinfeld: The bad object transference is most likely to occur full blown in psychotic, borderline, narcissistic, and schizoid conditions. However, these patients may on occasion manifest the bad object situation around oedipal level conflict as well. Also, a seemingly neurotic patient may present manifestations of the bad object on a higher developmental level. The following clinical example will illustrate this situation.

John applied for treatment because of a tendency to sabotage himself in love relationships and in his work life. He has just completed college, and he fears that he will screw himself up on his first job. John has been involved in the last few years in a steady relationship with a woman. He is concerned about his impulses to sleep with other women. In the past, he has fouled up relationships by sleeping with others and then telling his steady girlfriend out of guilt.

John quickly demonstrates his self-sabotaging tendencies. He oversleeps and fails to report to work. Johns says, "This is what I mean. I'm showing you what I do. I get something that would be good for me, then I screw it up. Then at work I find myself flirting with every woman. I'm thinking of how to seduce her. I'm not doing my work. I'm spending more and more time in the offices of my attractive coworkers. I only seek out the attractive ones. I never make friends with a woman who doesn't turn me on. I don't even talk to them. I never do any work. I'm always thinking of how to seduce. This is the way I'll screw up my job and my relationship with Patti. I do this kind of thing all the time. I can see it coming."

John is of Irish descent. He is the first member of his working-class family to receive a college education. His father left the family when John was five years old, and his mother was pregnant with his young brother. John's father was an alcoholic with poor work habits who ran around with other women. His mother became exasperated when his father repeatedly stayed out all night. She finally threw him out and refused a reconciliation. His father's life went down the drain, and he became a good-for-nothing bum.

John feels he is the apple of his mother's eye. His younger brother was a habitual drug user with poor work habits. John's mother is proud that he has managed to make something out of his life. When he brought her a plaque he had won for outstanding scholarly achievement, she hung it on her wall. But John also feels it is a bit strange that he surrendered it to his mother instead of keeping it himself. John wonders if his resentment about surrendering the plaque goes deeper. He states that he always felt he achieved everything for his mother. He would bring her all his good report cards and achievements from school, and she would say, when he did well, "You did that for Mommy. See how much Mommy loves you. You're my little man."

John has always been disturbed about his little man relationship to his mother. She never dated and never remarried. She referred to John as her little man, little lover, and little boyfriend. She said that she did not need a man, she needed only her children. John helped her take care of his little brother. Therefore, one aspect of John's relationship to his mother was his role as her little man, little lover, and little boyfriend who brought her his trophies and acted as a coparent to his brother. John felt

212

special and admired by his mother as her hero and her helper. She had dreams of success for him and often told him that when he grew up to be an important man, he could take care of her. The idea of being his mother's little man, hero, and helper excited and threatened John with incest.

However, this was only one side of his relationship to his mother. Often he would come very close to fulfilling some plan or hope she had for him but then sabotage his chances at the last minute. His mother would then say that she knows how brilliant he is and how well he could do but that he is lazy and no good like his father. I do not mean to suggest that the predominant characteristic of John's relationship to his mother was one of failing her; this dynamic characterized the younger brother's relationship to the mother for the most part, and John was the mother's successful, special child. Often enough, however, John would disappoint her just as he was on the verge of fulfilling one of her dreams. For instance, before embarking on his current career, he had pursued training in another area, but he had stopped training and dropped out right before completion. Now that John had finished his studies, he was frightened of failing again.

In becoming a lazy bum, John was bringing his internal father back on the scene. He would call himself a lazy bum who would never become anything, and his mother would join in and say he was exactly like his father. The identification with the loser father served as a buffer between the special, successful son and the admiring mother. The special son/loving mother were in essence interrupted by the unworthy father and denigrating mother. Internally, John ridiculed himself just as his mother berated his father, and he therefore sustained his internal relationship to his father. At the same time, in identifying with the abandoning father as a bum and then condemning that side of himself, he attacked the internal father. In denigrating himself as identified with the father, he kept alive his own relationship to a father who had abandoned him. He also sustained within himself the relationship between his mother and father, and he placed the internal parental relationship between the successful, special John and his loving mother.

In bringing his trophies to his mother, John was a special object to her, a precious phallus that she had always desired. While John's mother denigrated his father, she looked up to other idealized powerful men. She described her own father as a powerful, successful, self-made man. She wondered how she had found a man like her husband, weak and passive, exactly the opposite of her father. Before she met her husband, she had gone with another man, the love of her life, whom she had compared to her husband. She claimed never to have stopped loving this remarkable powerful former lover. Her ideal son repressed the powerful, bountiful successful former lover/father. John therefore often felt that he was the only love of his mother's life, that she admired him more than she loved his father, and that if he could only fulfill his mother's dreams for his success, the two of them would be emotionally married and live happily ever after. The incest taboo that John experienced at such direct oedipal wishes caused him to raise the specter of his father in identification between him and his mother. In sessions, the internalized split-off object relations units would become alternately manifested as he presented long monologues about his achievements at work and in winning the admiration of the various women in his life, only to interrupt himself with self-recriminations for messing up at work or wanting to seduce women other than Patti.

The foregoing comments describe John's internalized object relations from an oedipal point of view. However, these relations also enacted a significant pre-oedipal theme. John felt he had surrendered his autonomous achievements to his mother. He felt that she lived only for him, and there was much to this. Therefore, if he had kept his achievements solely for himself, his mother

214

would have felt threatened and abandoned. John could therefore be autonomous only if he surrendered the prizes of the other-than-mother world to his mother. But then he would begin to feel that she had castrated him or robbed him of his triumphs, and he would become enraged at her. John felt that his mother had robbed him of his autonomy, and therefore his "screwing up" behavior was his way of exacting revenge.

The transference was manifested in the following dream. As an adolescent, John had idolized rock star Bruce Springstein. In the dream, he meets his idol, but the star is in decline. Bruce has a long shaggy beard, he is very overweight, and his clothes are ragged. John feels sorry for Bruce and feels that he may not be aware of the terrible shape he is in. John decides not to tell him and to pretend to continue to look up to him. Then he awakens.

His first association is that Bruce does not have a beard but that I, the therapist, do. He can think of no further associations, so I ask him what brought about Bruce's decline in the dream. He immediately associates to Bruce's marital problems. He imagines that Bruce has left his wife and has gone into a decline. He is really unsure if Bruce is still living with his wife, but he imagines that the breakup of the marital relationship leading to Bruce's decline is significant. I ask whether that situation reminds him of anything in his own life, and he suddenly recalls the breakup of his parents' marriage and how his father became a bum. He then thinks how the dream signifies that he was going to hide from his father that the latter was losing the oedipal competition and was instead going to pretend to go on idealizing the father. Up to this point, the patient had idealized me as a "star therapist" and denied his competitive feelings, but the bad object transference finally emerged in the oedipal drama.

XI

Internalizing a Containing Object

This chapter will describe how the therapist enables a schizoid patient to internalize a containing object. Having had little experience with others who could contain their anxieties and distress, such patients often do not know how to make use of the therapy. The therapist must first demonstrate to the patient the ways in which he could potentially use the therapy for help and then clarify what gets in the way of his doing so.

RICHARD

The patient, Richard, is a businessman in his thirties. He initiated therapy because former wives and girlfriends complained that he did not share feelings, had little psychological insight, and could not give emotionally. Richard was married twice. His first wife complained that he was detached and miserly with money. He went to a therapist to appease her. He could find nothing to discuss, was blocked, and gained little insight. When his first wife

217

left, he quit therapy. The therapist interpreted that Richard attempted to make her feel abandoned as he had been made to feel by his wife. Richard said he did not feel abandoned and wondered if the therapist felt abandoned. When girlfriends and a second wife had the same complaints, he began to wonder if they were right. However, he was confused because he was always generous with his time and money.

Personal History

Richard grew up in an intact wealthy New England family. He had an older sister and younger brother. The siblings were married and successful professionals. Although he was successful in his career, Richard felt he had surrendered center stage to his siblings. His brother was a known professional athlete and very self-assured. His sister was a nationally known and prominent attorney. A cousin, Jennifer, had lived with the family after the death of her parents. She was Richard's age, and he thought of her as a half-sister. Jennifer was the only person Richard ever spoke to about his problems. She now lived alone and was depressed and lonely and sometimes called Richard for comfort. Richard was the most socially outgoing among his siblings. They had no personal friends and only knew people through work activities. Richard was not sociable by any standards, but he did have some friends and took part in school activities.

Richard described his mother as removed and self-absorbed. She met the material needs of the family but did not provide emotional support. If the children came to her with problems, she said, "Oh, come. You're not really upset. I know that can't bother you." Richard and his siblings complied. His cousin, Jennifer, remained troubled by the loss of her parents and problems at school. She returned home crying, complaining that peers picked on her. The mother replied, "Can't you leave me alone? You're so sensitive. There are enough troubles to deal with. Act your age."

Richard's father was described as a highly narcissistic man. He expressed a familial chauvinism, claiming they were superior in beauty, brains, and money. The parents referred to each other as the best mother and father.

Richard described his adolescence as uneventful. He performed adequately in high school and college. He joined up with local athletic and recreational activities and was friends with local peers. He was neither enthusiastic nor troubled with events in his life. There was one incident he recalled being excited about. He went on a camping trip with his senior class and met his first girlfriend. He was excited about being on his own, being with his first girl, exploring new territory. He described this adventure in our first session and clearly came to life. This liveliness was in contrast to his typical emotional constriction. He felt his life to be dull and uneventful. He had friends whom he did things with. They played sports, camped out, and more recently went to a bar for a beer and to watch a game.

In his relationships with women, he felt he could neither commit himself nor separate. There was one woman he lived with for a number of years. He provided for her materially and was agreeable about doing whatever she asked, but neither felt a strong emotional bond. He felt it was time to end the relationship but feared hurting her feelings. They could not decide to separate. They both had affairs. He realized that she became involved with someone to make him jealous. He was only a little upset but pretended that he was more upset than he was. She was pleased, and for a time they felt closer, but then it went back to how it was before. She had a second affair to end the relationship. He wondered why he did not leave her.

In his first marriage, he felt his wife was hysterical and demanding. He worried about money and making ends meet. She complained that he was cheap and cared only about money. He felt that she was unsympathetic to his financial needs. He earned a good living but could not live beyond his means. He did not feel that she was greedy for his money but rather that she did not know its value. He married a second time, and after four years his wife developed a terminal illness and died within a year. He completely devoted himself to taking care of her but actually felt detached. There were fleeting moments when grief overcame him, but then he felt numb. He recognized that the momentary grief had more to do with himself and a sudden infantile terror of being alone. As she lay dying, he was obsessed with expenses. In the first years of their marriage, she had complained of his lack of intimacy. However, once she became ill, she was grateful and moved by his devotion.

After his second wife died, he lived alone. He went through the motions of living, but with little vitality. At work, he did his job but avoided socializing. Friends and family left messages on his answering machine, and he sometimes did not respond. He felt basically uninterested in people. His colleagues sometimes invited him out for a drink, but he seldom went. He wondered what was lacking—was he antihuman, without ordinary feelings for people?

Question: What would prompt such an unrelated individual to seek treatment? He seems to believe that human relations are inevitably unsatisfactory. What, if any, understanding would he have of his own problems?

Seinfeld: Such patients often receive communication from others that something is wrong or missing. The individual may attempt to ask for a promotion at work. He might be told that he does his job correctly but that something is missing—a certain creativity or initiative or spirit. The patient gets the job done, but without any zest or vitality. Richard had a series of attachments in which he believed he fulfilled the role of lover or husband. However, his partners continually presented the same complaint: that he lacked a certain intimacy and energy. After hearing a series of individuals present similar complaints, he started to believe that something was missing, a certain vitality, spontaneity, and energy that is indicative of the true self.

Question: How does the therapist work with something missing? Ordinarily, we think of the therapist working with something present persecuting the patient: bad objects, conflicts, anxiety, depression.

Seinfeld: This is correct. The therapist focuses on what was omitted in development. The intervention does not uncover conflict but rather addresses deficits in parenting that result in deficiency of ego functioning. George Frank (personal communication) pointed out that the patient cannot exercise weak or nonexistent ego functions until he is aware they are missing.

In the beginning of treatment, Richard repeatedly voiced anxiety over having nothing to say. He discussed the problems and his history and expressed concerns that he was not delving deeply in the matters, only the past and present everyday facts of life. I responded that such issues were important in their own right and that the deep issues are not tapped until the groundwork is done. I said, "They are not reached by a strained effort. It is best to go into whatever is on your mind, even if it seems trivial, irrelevant, and superficial, and let deep things come of their own accord."

When he expressed anxiety that he would not have anything to say, I did not explore or interpret resistance but instead provided holding. "So far you have had things to say." He acknowledged having more to say than expected, and I said, "It is my sense that there has been something to say, so why shouldn't it continue?"

Richard's narrative suggested that he experienced himself as more of an object and not as a subject. Feelings, thoughts, and life events were experienced more as happening to him than as being created by him. Ogden points out that the person who experiences himself as an object lacks the capacity to symbolize and relates on a concrete level with little insight. Thus, if Richard described how a woman was angry with him because he did not share his feelings or have insight, I did not interpret his fear of intimacy or withholding as aggression but instead remarked on his dilemma of being asked to do something he had no capacity to do.

Richard's lifelong impoverishment of object relations suggested that he lacked the experience of a good containing object. Bion described how the infant uses projective identification to communicate disruptive, overwhelming feelings. The mothering figure serves as a container through her reverie, thereby metabolizing the feelings that then become manageable for the infant. Fairbairn believed that the infant may retain psychic contents because of a fear of loss. Self-expression may be experienced as expulsion of an internal object. Evacuation may be not only the wish to be rid of an object but also an effort to give. Bringing together Bion's and Fairbairn's views, it seems to me that internal

222

contents can be given and are not lost only if there is a good containing object to give them to. The retention of contents reflects the struggle to retain the internal object in spite of aggression and tenuous object constancy. It would therefore be foolhardy to interpret resistance and elicit aggression. Instead, I focused on the deficit of a good containing object. Richard often remarked that he feared he was empty-headed and had nothing to say.

> *Therapist:* It's my sense that it's not that you are empty-headed.
>
> *Richard:* (laughing) I'm afraid maybe there is nothing there. Hollow. No feelings, thoughts, or ideas.
>
> *Therapist:* I think it's important to look at precisely what is lacking. In our sessions, with a little help, you have had something to say about yourself, your life, and other people.
>
> *Richard:* That's true.
>
> *Therapist:* Therefore, I believe it isn't that there is nothing there but rather you are afraid of losing what there is so you withhold self-expression.
>
> *Richard:* What do you mean—losing what is there?
>
> *Therapist:* That thoughts and feelings are kept from your consciousness, so you are not needing to express them.

Here I spoke to Richard in the mode of self as object. I did not say, "You keep thoughts and feelings from consciousness," because it was too removed from his experience of being the object of his thoughts and feelings.

> *Richard:* So you are saying it is not just that I am hollow or superficial. Is there a reason for this?
>
> *Therapist:* There is something I have in mind. When someone tells another person about an important experience or

feeling or idea and the other person doesn't listen, misunderstands, or does not care, it can feel that whatever is expressed is lost, disappears into a vacuum. The other person does not recognize it as important; it loses its value and becomes meaningless.

Richard: Are there people who actually like to communicate? (laughs)

Therapist: Let's think about it. If the other person values what is said, takes it in, considers it, then gives feedback, it is not lost. Rather, it is returned with a dividend. What is given is returned—with a bonus. What the other puts into it. The recognition.

Here again I was careful not to discuss Richard as a subject intentionally acting. Rather, I described the experience in terms of what was done to him or how it would be experienced by him.

Richard became aware that he did not retain our discussions. The inability to remember was another indication of the deficit of a containing object. Not until he had a sense that the therapist valued and contained what was said would Richard begin to hold on to what he said.

Richard: Where are we? I do not recall what was said last time.

Therapist: Maybe if you think about it. (silence) Do you recall?

Richard: Let's see. It's a blank.

Therapist: What made you think of it? Was what you were thinking related to it?

After allowing some time to remember, I mentioned one issue we had discussed to stimulate his evocative memory. I mentioned something rather innocuous to provide him with an opportunity to recall what was significant. He expressed wonder when I remembered. My aim was to provide him with the experience of a containing object so that he could identify with this function and begin to value and contain his own contents.

Question: What you are describing here as internalizing a containing object sounds identical to the ego psychology notion of object constancy. It is the same—what is the relationship?

Seinfeld: Object constancy refers to internalizing a positive, comforting image of the object while recognizing that the object sometimes frustrates and is not always available. Containing refers to the object taking in the patient's overwhelming, distressing affect. These two concepts are related. If the patient does not believe the object contains the patient's distress, the patient will not be motivated to internalize a positive image of the object. Instead, he will internalize the object as a faulty container.

Question: How do patient and therapist begin to recognize failures in containing?

Seinfeld: The therapist must help the patient recognize some of the underlying reasons for the patient's avoidance of human contact. Richard did not return phone calls or letters and avoided people at work. I explored this further and learned that he often received negative input from people.

> *Richard:* Bill, the friend I've mentioned, left a hundred messages. (laughs) I'm exaggerating.
> *Therapist:* Tell me about your relationship with Bill.

Discussing their friendship, he made passing mention that Bill often offered unsolicited advance. When I brought this dissatisfaction to his attention, Richard said the person whose letters he did not answer was often highly critical. Richard added that during the week, he was depleted from working overtime every night. He called his brother and complained about how tired he was. He replied, "Well, you're getting paid, right?"

Ordinarily, such a remark would not have disturbed him. He was now aware of wanting some empathic recognition. He realized that not too long ago, he would not have complained to his brother. There was never any expectation of an empathic response. He realized that when he was growing up, no one was permitted to complain. "My parents made you feel that you were an emotional weakling if you asked for anything."

Question: It sounds as if he has internalized the rejection of his own need for human contact as a weakness. How do you work with this as his need for recognition becomes stronger?

Seinfeld: Richard felt that he should be mature, force himself to go to a museum, read about art, and meet new and mature people. His former therapist had encouraged him to face the social situations he feared. I asked him how this had worked out. He said he had tried but had not felt true to his self and had not become more sociable. He did have a greater need for human contact but felt it was not constructive. I asked why, and he said he felt lonely and thought of contacting an old friend but that the friend was childlike, never assumes responsibility, and only likes to play, whether it is sports, games, or the computer. Richard felt that they were like children together and that probably it was not good. I remarked that just as his friend was always a child, Richard played at being an adult and never let himself feel childlike. His effort at assuming the role of an adult felt forced because he denied the need to play. He felt it was weak and immature to play. I said that there was a difference between letting go of responsibilities for a weekend and doing so permanently. He could consider what activity he really wanted to do—learning about art, going to a museum, and meeting new people could be enjoyable, but so could visiting an old friend and playing.

As Richard felt the need for more contact, his antilibidinal identification with the rejecting parental object was activated. He rejected his own need for contact as weak, and he admonished himself to act maturely. I did not yet interpret this but instead provided a holding explanation that alluded to the true and false self, the positive value of play, and emphasized that he could make a choice on the basis of his own needs.

Question: In your writings about the schizoid patient, you have said that things sometimes replace people. Was this characteristic present in your work with Richard? If so, how was it addressed?

Seinfeld: Richard expressed interest in understanding his past relationships with women. He became aware that he had trouble not only in accepting empathy but also in giving to the other. He had always been generous with his time, help, and money, but he lacked the capacity for emotional concern. He described the women in his life with little emotional differentiation. The breaking off of his relationship with his first wife was revealing of his difficulties with intimacy. As the relationship ended, he felt no feelings of sadness, anger, or loss but became concerned only with spending or losing money far beyond any realistic consideration. He was able to see that he had displaced his anxiety over the loss of the relationship onto the loss of money.

227

Bowlby described how children exposed to traumatic separation anxiety substitute possession of nonhuman things for disappointing human relations. The self, lacking recognition, experiences a sense of emptiness. The subject may seek to fill the lack by acquisition of possessions. Acquisition is a way to feel substantial. Richard responded to disappointments in human relations by fortifying himself with possessions.

Richard recalled that when his first wife left him and they kissed good-bye, he looked over her shoulder at the apartment, thinking it was urgently in need of repair. He had no feelings about the breakup with his wife. He worked furiously on the apartment for several weeks to the point of exhaustion and near collapse. Richard was able to see that his urgent need to repair the broken-up apartment was a metaphor for his need to repair the broken-up internal relationship.

Question: In object relations therapy, the therapeutic relationship is often considered to be the medium for enabling the patient to overcome a deficit in object relations. How do you enable as detached a patient as Richard to focus on the therapeutic relationship?

Seinfeld: This is a slow process requiring much patience. The therapist begins by paying close attention to the patient's reactions to any disruption in the treatment and sensitivity to feeling rejected.

I took a vacation after treating Richard for only a few months. When I returned and explored his reaction, he acknowledged feeling less connected. It felt like beginning all over again. Before the vacation, I had explored whether he ever thought about what we discussed between sessions. He said he had not, that he never thought of doing so. After our discussion, he had begun to think of what we discussed for a day or two after the session. Now that I returned from the vacation, he reverted back to that state. I interpreted that he may have been angry at me for going away and evacuated me from his mind. This interpretation was probably premature. It was more useful when I provided a holding revelation of the deficit. "You are not accustomed to getting anything of value from people. It is not surprising that you can't hold on to feelings about relationships."

I made several similar interventions, and he began to think of what we discussed as he had before. He thought of calling his friend Anna. She was mature, accepting, and caring. Their relationship was not romantic in that Anna had a boyfriend. He could not bring himself to call. When he considered doing so, the need left him. He suddenly became lethargic. I pointed out to him that this mood came over him just when he wanted to call so that something in him may have created the mood. He recalled that as he deliberated about calling Anna, he was thinking of our previous session, when he had said he fears expressing his feelings to people because they might reject him. However, he experienced the thoughts about Anna and the thoughts about our session as going along two different tracks. He was surprised that he did not put together the simple ideas that he avoided calling Anna because he feared she might reject him. It was unusual for Richard to take the initiative when he got together with people; it was almost always at their initiative.

Bion described the schizoid patient's attack on linking in their thought processes. The patient attacks cause and effect and other associative phenomena. The schizoid patient suffers overwhelming envy over dependence on the breast. Richard, an obsessive-compulsive neurotic with an underlying schizoid core, was not as severely disturbed as the patients described by Bion. Nevertheless, he displayed attacks on linking.

Question: Schizoid patients are often described as having false-self accommodations to others in their mode of object relating. How did this mode play out in Richard's concerns about rejection? How is this false-self accommodation addressed in treatment?

Seinfeld: Richard became more aware of what occurred in his object relationships. There were occasions when he spoke to someone, considered the discussion ridiculous, and then was surprised when the other seemed to enjoy the contact. He imagined that the other interacted only out of a sense of obligation. Richard then made himself agreeable so the other would be less put off. He acknowledged that he related to others mostly out of a sense of obligation. I therefore interpreted that his view of the other as relating only out of obligation was colored by his own experience. We realized that this situation replicated his own family history. Whenever he had asked his parents for anything, they had been self-absorbed and treated him as a bother. They had not rejected his wishes outright, given that it was important for them to live up to their ideal of good parents, but had responded with a sense of obligation.

Over the next few weeks, Richard became more aware of his sense of obligation and accommodation. He felt he no longer wanted to accommodate others. He felt he always went along with what others wished or wanted and experienced no pleasure for himself. This is what created tension in his relationships with others and resulted in his wish to avoid most people. He felt withdrawn and that he had nothing to give. He felt lonely but did not make contact. I said that his statement that he had nothing to give assumed that the other wanted something. I said, "Your idea of the other person is that he demands, and therefore relating is giving yourself over."

He became more animated than usual in response and recalled various ways he had to be helpful and give himself over in childhood. He then described how, when people call him, he feels not only burdened but also angry, thinking they should leave him be. I remarked that the theme was of being intruded on. He said this was not entirely on the right track. His parents were not so much intrusive as wanting to be left alone. In exploring being left alone, he discussed how he and his brother shared a large room.

> *Therapist:* How old were you?
> *Richard:* Always. From the time I was born. It was strange. My parents were not poor. It was the idea that we should not get in our parents' hair. We were independent. We played by ourselves for hours. My mother always boasted about how we could be left alone because we entertained ourselves. It was not that we were deprived. At least, not in the usual way. There were a million things to play with and do. There was also a tutor—a helper who organized our activities. It was all very structured. The adults set the stage, and we carried on as expected.

Some children may be overly patterned by their environment. They become precociously independent as they fit into prepatterned programmed experience. Richard's overly accommodating behavior appeared to be based on a lifelong experience of accommodating to a familial situation with little opportunity to express his needs.

Question: So far, you have discussed this patient in terms of deficits in object relating. What about conflictual defenses, such as projective identification? Do schizoid patients project object relations conflicts: If so, when and how does the clinician respond?

Seinfeld: It is true that during the first year, my interventions focused on holding and recognition of deficits and impaired object relations. Richard's description of others gave increasing recognition of projective identification. For instance, Richard described colleagues at work expressing frustration that he never socialized with them. His laughter about their efforts indicated that he enjoyed their frustration.

> *Richard:* What should I do? Should I force myself to be sociable?
> *Therapist:* Have you tried this?
> *Richard:* Yes.
> *Therapist:* How did it work?
> *Richard:* It didn't.
> *Therapist:* You are putting into me that part of yourself that wants you to be more social. You are wanting me to play the part of encouraging you to be more social. When you don't respond to your colleagues at work who attempt to engage you, you have them play this role. I'm not saying you do this on purpose. Instead of feeling the conflict of relating or not relating, you induce others to want you to relate so you can only experience the unrelated part.

I did not make this interpretation all at once. As he described various experiences of others feeling rejected by him, I tried to stimulate his curiosity about his lack of such feelings and his disinterest in contact. Although he did not yet feel this to be true, he became curious.

Richard witnessed a fight between a couple. One person demanded more attention from the other. Richard felt anger at the individual demanding attention but recognized that his anger was out of proportion to the situation. He recalled feeling angry at former girlfriends he described as needy. I remarked that the girlfriend may represent the mother of his childhood who needed and demanded his attention but seldom nurtured him. He said he never wants anything from his mother. She recently called and asked why he never calls or visits. I said he might be avenging himself on her for rejecting his need for primary love. He did so by communicating, "If you will not give me what I want, then I will not need anything. I reject you as you reject me."

In this way, he rejected not only his mother but also his own dependency on her. The sadism he felt seeing friends and colleagues frustrated reflected his fantasy of turning the table on his mother for rejecting him. One day, he came in with material that confirmed this conflict. He had visited friends who had a baby. When the baby cried and demanded, he felt angry. He imagined the baby being stomped on. He also felt angry at the mother for being so tolerant of the baby's crying. He believed the mother was spoiling the baby, creating an insatiable monster. He acknowledged knowing very little about their relationship and recognized that his strong response had to do with his own inner issues. I remarked that this situation of an angry, rejecting attitude toward a crying baby was going on inside him all the time. It was usually outside his awareness unless an external situation triggered the conflict. I added that repression of this conflict permitted him to remain in contact with the world in a cool, detached manner. If he allowed the conflict expression, it would disturb the minimal contact he had with the outer world. He thought about this and said, "So I withdraw in order to stay in contact."

The next week, Richard came in and said that his life was like a sugar-free, fat-free yogurt.

Therapist: What is that like?

Richard: As food it's great for the body. But it is not good if your life is that way. Kind of pure, ideal but sterile, without passion or zest. My relationships are superficial. I understand last week that this is how I live emotionally. Very bland. I like to do outdoor activities. But the most I ever do is drive to the woods—the same place all of the time—and walk. It is a beautiful park. When I am with my girlfriend, we do nothing but watch television. We only go out if she initiates it. Then, she complains of my austerity. I would prefer the most economical of restaurants, the cheapest wine. She said I'm always holding back, while I say she is extravagant with my money.

Therapist: What do you think of your difference?

Richard: There is probably truth to both of our views.

Richard began to question his mode of relating. He said he may be giving a wrong impression. Although he picks the most modest places for pleasure, it is not that he is cheap. He would often give much materially even though he worried about his expenditures. In fact, previous girlfriends often accused him of being cheap emotionally, not materially. He began to think of what former girlfriends said because he had a new woman in his life and did not wish to destroy the relationship.

Object relations theory suggests that giving is the mature mode of relating. Originally, the infant relates by taking, but later it is inclined to give or give back. There is an evolutionary basis to this development in that mutual cooperation and reciprocity of giving supports the survival of the species. Therefore, I initially emphasized the adaptive side of his giving by saying, "The fact that you can give is a strength. It shows concern and is your way of connecting. But let's see if there is a problematic side to it." Through exploration, Richard realized that he sometimes provided help when the other did not need it. I said his caring seemed to be related not only to his caring but also to insecurity. Initially, Richard's giving behavior was understood as a false-self accommodation to the object he obliged. There was now a depressive aspect present.

Question: You seem to suggest that the depressive aspect indicates progress over the false-self accommodation. Can you explain this in developmental terms? What are the dynamics involved, and how is this manifested clinically?

Seinfeld: The depressive position implies the recognition of separation and loss and the wish to make reparation toward one's ambivalently loved object. This manic defense against this position involves omnipotently controlling the object to deny separation, loss. As Richard improved, the theme of loss emerged. His new girlfriend planned an airplane trip. She did not have much money. There was discussion of Richard's paying for the trip. She was ambivalent about asking for help. In the past, he would have taken over the entire trip, planning it and paying for it. He was now reluctant to do so; they discussed the issue further, and she said she would like to pay for part of her own way. For the first time, he experienced separation anxiety and worried that she might meet a man on the trip. Richard realized that by taking over the trip, he attempted to control her to avoid the risk of losing her. In such situations, he would become resentful because he expected the girlfriend to comply with all his wishes, and when she eventually could not live up to this, he felt taken advantage of.

Richard now recalled that when he was six months old, his parents took a vacation abroad for several weeks. He had always been told that his parents described him as a perfect baby who did not protest. Although he could not remember the incident, he became angry and saddened that his parents were so detached as to leave him at such a vulnerable time. He felt that if they had been as excited about caring for him, they would not have left. He understood that his lifelong need to accommodate and give to others was a defense against loss.

As he struggled with these depressive themes, he felt guilt over the unhappiness of his second wife. He felt that she had been serious about having a close and meaningful life with him but that he did not have the capacity to love. When she became ill, he detached himself. He wished he could communicate to her his understanding of her pain and disappointment. In fantasy, he made reparation by imaging what he wished he could say. This sadness over his second wife was also a reliving of the early loss of his mother.

For the first time, Richard felt a need to tell others of his feelings of loss. He had told his sister, a friend, and his girlfriend. This was definitely a new feeling—to release painful emotions. The stress affected him physically. His stomach was upset, and he suffered from diarrhea. He also felt mildly depressed. He described diarrhea as getting rid of the junk he hated. I also pointed out that he was feeling a need to get rid of troubling emotions. I reminded him of our earliest discussions about holding on to painful emotions. I said that now his ridding himself of these emotions about people was a form of separation and loss and caused him to feel depressed. I said that at the same time, he is not just losing his feelings because there is now the idea of sharing them with others since he wants to express his feelings to significant people.

Richard wondered if he was just dumping his feelings onto others. He said that he read a magazine about people who narcissistically unloaded feelings. Although he had never before heard of this idea, it resonated with some of what he felt when he expressed himself. He thought about this and said it was not only that he wished to get rid of the feelings; he also wanted to talk them over with other people but that getting rid of was the dominant emotion. He said he was not able to think of a full give-and-take with another person. I then asked if there was a reason that he selected the particular persons he spoke to. He said all of them listened sympathetically. I pointed out that there was a change: He now had the idea of a caring listener to whom he could give his inner contents. The feelings could be expressed without being lost.

Question: The schizoid individual is so closed down to his dependency needs. How do these needs become manifest in the transference, and how does the patient become involved with such fears of loss?

Seinfeld: Often the dependency needs at first emerge as split off. The therapist has to actively listen for remarks about others that could refer to him. If this becomes a pattern, then there is evidence that dependency has emerged but is being split off. The therapist has to decide when the patient will be ready for interpretation of splitting.

Richard reported that on his way to the sessions, he passed a nearby hospital and thought of the medical care in the city. There was a man standing outside the hospital appearing forlorn and lost. Richard imagined that he was a patient in need of help. Richard felt relieved that he was not in the man's place. He imagined him to be homeless. Earlier during the week, Richard had been to his HMO for a checkup. He expected to be in and out quickly. The waiting room had been full of people he imagined to be on welfare or mentally ill. He was annoyed at having to wait. He thought that these bureaucratic systems kept the poor and indigent in dependent, helpless positions. He imagined that the clinic provided unnecessary tests and excited endless need by doling out welfare. He believed the helpers did not really care. The staff probably did not consider a middle-class person like himself as very important when they had so many needy people. He imagined the staff was too overwhelmed to properly care for him.

I remarked that he complained about poor treatment and not receiving proper attention because the physicians were overwhelmed by needier patients. I pointed out that he also came for treatment and wondered if he ever felt this way about therapy. He said that his feelings about therapy were not at all related to his feelings about the clinic or hospital. He believed I paid attention and was not overwhelmed. I raised the possibility that the needy patients could stand for the dependent side of himself, whereas I could stand for the bureaucratic, overwhelmed physician who excited but does not meet his dependency needs. He felt no awareness of this state and instead believed his attitude to our relationship to be detached, rational, and professional. I agreed that it was but reminded him that in his story he was rejecting toward the needy and the system and that it was possible that he similarly rejected those feelings in our relationship and that was why he had no awareness of them. This idea interested him intellectually and he replied, "So then I would have two relationships with you—the cooperative one I'm aware of and the other in which I'm dependent and frustrated." I said that would be correct and, if so, that he rejected the needy, dependent component. He said our cooperative relationship did not feel false. He was involved, he tried to understand himself, and the therapy was helpful. He admitted that this description was rather ideal. I acknowledged that our cooperative relationship was not false, that he tried to understand himself, and that we had a strong working alliance. I said if the therapy is working this way and was helpful, he would feel irrational if he allowed for the dependent, frustrated feelings that he likened to the needy patients at his clinic.

He understood my remarks and said that when he awakened that morning, he thought he had nothing to discuss in therapy that day. Walking to the session, he thought of his first wife. He recalled the ways they had disappointed and frustrated each other. It was at this point that he passed the hospital, saw the forlorn patient, and recalled his visit to the HMO. I said the unconscious is nearest expression on awakening because dreaming is the state where it reigns. I said that it was possible that his thought about having nothing to say today may have been an unconscious command not to say or think anything. Thinking of his first wife, the hospital clinic, and the needy patient may have all indicated that the needy, dependent self was seeking some expression that could disrupt his ideal, cooperative relationship to me. If it could be kept down, unheard and unfelt, he could continue to receive the ideal treatment without it getting in the way.

He did not feel any of those dependent feelings. Nevertheless, the ideas interested him. In a philosophical, detached manner, he said he thought there could be some truth to my remarks. He said he would allow himself to further pursue these thoughts but wanted to make sure I knew he did not experience these needs. I assured him that I was aware that he did not.

He thought of what could be the origin of these theoretically disowned feelings. He said that his family life had, in many ways, been a bureaucracy. He and his siblings were provided with many things. Their activities were always patterned and structured, yet they had been shown little care or attention. I remarked that he grew up repressing the dissatisfaction and anger over this state of affairs in order to get along in his family. Therapy, being a helping relationship, can awaken unmet early needs. The object of his needs was a bureaucratic family that did not respond. I said that when the object of one's needs is experienced as exciting, frustrating, rejecting, and bad, the needs themselves are experienced that way. The entire situation is repressed—needs, objects, and all. Richard said that my idea would explain how he experienced the world as "sugar-free, fat-free, plain yogurt."

Richard said, "I find your idea strangely reassuring. If I have repressed all these feelings, it would explain why I'm so detached, and it would mean I'm not simply a bland person by nature."

Question: How would Richard's schizoid way of relating in the world be understood in terms of Guntrip's concept of a regressed, passive ego? Guntrip believed that the core of the schizoid condition was a regressed ego that has split off from the active, dependent frustrated ego that you have described in this continuing discussion of Richard. Is Guntrip's concept relevant here?

Seinfeld: Very much so. Guntrip argued that impingement and neglect were likely to result in a regressed, passive ego, while overstimulation and overt rejection were likely to result in the active oral-sadomasochistic ego. Richard suffered primarily from early neglect and impingement, giving rise to the regressed and withdrawn libidinal ego. Throughout his childhood, Richard allowed his siblings and parents to take center stage. His younger brother and father were highly aggressive and competitive, reminding him of his first wife. In the family, he stepped aside as everyone fought and competed for scarce, needed emotional supplies. He recalled being on a train and seeing several youths who, he imagined, lived in the suburbs. All but one boy were loud and lively, laughing and kidding. The one youth stood to the side, dressed in casual clothes like the others but withdrawn and not taking part in the horsing around. Richard was like this youth— part of the group yet emotionally outside. A part of him was there, but a deeper part was not fully present.

Toward the end of the second year of treatment, I took a vacation. Richard visited his friends at the same time. He reported that his friends were extremely competitive. They competed with talking, debating, and playing baseball, volleyball, and Frisbee. Whenever he saw them, their entire time was spent in competition. In the past, he always played halfheartedly; somewhat withdrawn when they talked, they did not allow each other to get a word in edgewise. There was an oral quality as if a group of children were grabbing at urgently needed food. For the first time, he insisted on his say and did not stand over on the side. When they played ball, he also did his best. In the past, he had always felt passive, weak, and tired. Now, he had energy and aggression.

Question: What are some of the indications of personality growth in the work with schizoid patients?

Seinfeld: Such patients often do not take initiative in establishing relationships if relationships follow rigid social role prescriptions. There is a retreat into familiar, safe physical surroundings and an attraction to abstract ideas devoid of emotionally meaningful impact. Richard began to initiate relationships and developed the capacity for loneliness. His outdoor interests expanded as he learned to sail and ski and took trips he had previously fantasized about. In relationships with women, even if he was certain that he and the other were not right for each other, he never initiated separation but rather provoked or waited for the other to leave him. Although he certainly still had difficulty with intimacy, he started to date a variety of women, attempted to discover what characteristics he liked and disliked, sensitively separated from some relationships, and tolerated rejection when on the receiving end. In all, Richard is becoming more related and autonomous and less passive and withdrawn.

References

Abraham, K. (1919). A particular form of neurotic resistance against the psychoanalytic method. In *Selected Papers of Karl Abraham*, pp. 303–311. New York: Brunner/Mazel, 1927.

Barrett, W. (1979). *The Illusion of Technique*. New York: Anchor.

Bion, W. (1984). *Learning from Experience*, pp. 31–37. London: Maresfield.

Buber, M. (1958). *I and Thou*. New York: Scribner.

Campbell, J. (1949). *The Hero with a Thousand Faces*, pp. 49–148. Princeton, NJ: Bollinger Series.

Eigen, M. (1993a). Catastrophe and faith. In *The Electrified Tightrope: Selected Papers of Michael Eigen*, ed. A. Phillips, Northvale, NJ: Jason Aronson.

Fairbairn, W. R. D. (1941). A revised psychopathology of the psychoses and psychoneuroses. In *Psychoanalytic Studies of the Personality*, pp. 28–58. London: Routledge & Kegan Paul, 1952.

Fairbairn, W. R. D. (1943). The repression and return of bad objects. In *Psychoanalytic Studies of the Personality*, pp. 59–81. London: Routledge & Kegan Paul, 1952.

Fairbairn, W. R. D. (1944). Endopsychic structure considered in terms of object relationships. In *Psychoanalytic Studies of the Personality*, pp. 82–136. London: Routledge & Kegan Paul, 1952.

Fairbairn, W. R. D. (1958). On the nature and aims of psycho-analytic treatment. *International Journal of Psycho-Analysis* 39:374–385.

Ferenczi, S. (1933). Confusion of tongues between adult and child. In *Final Contributions to the Problem of Methods of Psycho-analysis*, ed. M. Balint. New York: Basic Books, 1955.

Freud, S. (1916). Some character types met with in psychoanalytic work. In *Collected Papers*, vol. 4, pp. 318–344. New York: Basic Books, 1959.

Freud, S. (1917). Mourning and melancholia. In *Collected Papers*, vol. 4, pp. 152–172. New York: Basic Books, 1959.

Freud, S. (1924). The economic problem in masochism. In *Collected Papers*, vol. 2, pp. 255–268. New York: Basic Books, 1959.

Freud, S. (1937). Analysis terminable and interminable. In *Collected Papers*, vol. 5, pp. 316–357. New York: Basic Books, 1959.

Grotstein, J. (1985). *Splitting and Projective Identification*, p. 164. New York: Jason Aronson.

Guntrip, H. (1969). *Schizoid Phenomena, Object Relations and the Self*. New York: International Universities Press.

Jacobson, E. (1964). The fusion between self and object images and the earliest types of identifications. In *The Self and the Object World*, pp. 33–48. New York: International Universities Press.

Kernberg, O. (1975). The syndrome. In *Borderline Conditions and Pathological Narcissism*, pp. 3–48. New York: Jason Aronson.

Klein, M. (1946). Notes on some schizoid mechanisms. In *Envy and Gratitude and Other Works, 1946–1963*, pp. 122–140. New York: Delta, 1975.

Klein, M. (1957). Envy and gratitude. In *Envy and Gratitude and Other Works, 1946–1963*, pp. 136–275. New York: Delta, 1975.

Klein, M. (1959). Our adult world and its roots in infancy. In *Envy and Gratitude and Other Works, 1946–1963*, London: Virago Press, 1988.

Kohut, H. (1971). *The Analysis of the Self.* New York: International Universities Press.

Mahler, M., Pine, F. & Bergman, A. (1975). The Psychological Birth of the Human Infant. Hutchinson.

McDougall, J. (1980). *Plea for a Measure of Abnormality.* Madison, CN: International Universities Press.

Ogden, T. (1986). *The Matrix of the Mind: Object Relations and the Psychoanalytic Dialogue.* Northvale, NJ: Jason Aronson.

Racher, H. (1968). *Transference and countertransference.* London: Hogarth Press and the Institute of Psycho-Analysis.

Rosenfeld, Harold. (1987). Narcissistic patients with negative therapeutic reactions. In *Impasse and Interpretation,* pp. 85–104. London: Tavistock.

Searles, H. (1961). Phases of patient-therapist interaction in the psychotherapy of chronic schizophrenia. In *Collected Papers on Schizophrenia and Relation Subjects,* pp. 521–559. New York: International Universities Press.

Searles, H. (1967). Concerning the development of an identity. *Psychoanalytic Review,* 53:507–520, 1967.

Seinfeld, J. (1991). *The Empty Core.* Northvale, NJ: Jason Aronson.

Sutherland, J. (1989). *Fairbairn's Journey into the Interior,* London: Free Association Books.

Sutherland, J. D. (1994a). The autonomous self. In *The Autonomous Self: The Work of John D. Sutherland,* ed. J. S. Scharff, pp. 303–330. Northvale, NJ: Jason Aronson.

Winnicott, D. W. (1958). The capacity to be alone. In *The Maturational Processes and the Facilitating Environment,* pp. 29–36. New York: International Universities Press, 1965.

Winnicott, D. W. (1960). The theory of the parent-infant relationship. In *Maturational Processes and the Facilitating Environment,* pp. 37–55. New York: International Universities Press, 1965.

Winnicott, D. W. (1963). Dependence in infant care, in child care, and in the psychoanalytic setting. In *Maturational Processes and the Fascilitating Environment,* pp. 249–250. New York: International Universities Press, 1965.

Winnicott, D. W. (1971). *Playing and Reality.* London: Tavistock.

Index

Bad object (*cont.*)
  rejection, 126–127, 138–
    139, 140–143
  severe ego weakness,
    130–132
  split-off bad object trans-
    ference, 127–129
  splitting in the transference,
    134–138
  transference-
    countertransference
    issues, 132–134,
    139–140
Barrett, W., 87
Bion, Wilfred, 8, 26, 222, 229

Campbell, J., 63
Children, negative therapeutic
    reaction treatment of, 153
  children's loyalty to bad
    objects, 24
  early principles of child
    therapy, 153–155
  ego-supportive techniques/
    approach, 154–156,
    162–164
  internal object relations, 168
  manifestations in children,
    157–159
  method of engagement in
    treatment process,
    160–162
  Robert case report, 159–160

  self and object relations
    theory, 156–157
  transference-
    countertransference
    issues, 164–168
  Yvette case report, 169–171
Clinical diagnosis, 7
Complementary identification,
    26
Concordant identification, 26
Containing object, internalizing
    a, 217
  acquisition of possessions,
    227–228
  dependency needs, 237–240
  false-self accommodation,
    230–231, 235–237
  object constancy, 225
  patient's need for recogni-
    tion, 226–227
  personality growth, 241
  projective identification,
    231–235
  recognizing failures in con-
    taining, 225–226
  regressed, passive ego,
    240–241
  Richard case report,
    217–221
  therapeutic relationship,
    228–229
  working with something
    missing, 221–225

About the Author

Jeffrey Seinfeld, Ph.D., is a full-time professor at New York University School of Social Work and a private consultant of the Jewish Board of Family and Children's Service. Dr. Seinfeld is a Scientific Member of the Object Relations Institute. He received his Ph.D. from New York University of Social Work and his M.S.W. from Hunter College of Social Work. He has authored and co-edited works in the fields of psychotherapy and clinical social work, including *Interpreting and Holding: The Paternal and Maternal Functions of the Psychotherapist*, *The Bad Object: Handling the Negative Therapeutic Reaction in Psychotherapy*, and *The Empty Core: An Object Relations Approach to Psychotherapy of the Schizoid Personality*. Dr. Seinfeld is in the private practice of psychotherapy in New York City.